The Navy that Beat Napoleon

Walter Brownlee
MASTER MARINER

CAMBRIDGE UNIVERSITY PRESS
Cambridge
London   New York   New Rochelle
Melbourne   Sydney

Published by the Press Syndicate of the University of Cambridge
The Pitt Building, Trumpington Street, Cambridge CB2 1RP
32 East 57th Street, New York, NY 10022, USA
296 Beaconsfield Parade, Middle Park, Melbourne 3206, Australia

First published 1980

Printed in Great Britain by
Ebenezer Baylis & Son Ltd, The Trinity Press,
Worcester and London

Library of Congress cataloguing in publication data
Brownlee, Walter, 1930–
The navy that beat Napoleon.

(Cambridge introduction to the history of mankind: Topic book)

SUMMARY: Describes the ships, the men, and the main strategies
and campaigns of the British navy that defeated the French in the
Napoleonic wars.

1. Great Britain–History, Naval–18th century–Juv. lit. 2. Great
Britain–History, Naval–19th century–Juv. lit. 3. Great Britain.
Navy–History–Juv. lit. 4. France–History, Military–1789-1815–
Juv. lit. 5. Naval art and science–History–Juv. lit. [1. Great Britain.
Navy–History. 2. France–History, Military–1789-1815. 3. Naval art
and science–History] I. Title.
DA87.B84   1979   359′00941   78-18091
ISBN 0 521 22145 5

**Maps, drawings and diagrams by
Peter Dennis, Reg Piggott and Peter North**

The author and publisher would like to thank the following for
permission to reproduce illustrations:

front cover, pp 1, 8 (bottom left), 17, 18, 19, 21, 26, 34, 37, 42 (right),
43, 44, 46, back cover National Maritime Museum, London; p 4
Guildhall Library, City of London; p 6 Photographie Bulloz; p 8
(top left) Science Museum, London; p 8 (top right) British Library;
pp 11, 13, 22 (left) photographs by Naval photographer, reproduced
by kind permission of the Commanding Officer H.M.S. *Victory*; p 15
National Motor Museum; p 22 (right), 48 photographs Cambridge
University Library; pp 27, 33, 42 (left), 42 (centre) Mansell
Collection.

front cover: *The scene on the deck of* Victory *when Nelson fell,
painted by D. Dighton (1792–1827). The view is from the
forward rail of the poop deck, looking forward, and shows the
quarter deck, the covered waist, and the forecastle. Many such
scenes were painted by artists ashore attempting to recreate the
frantic activity and tension of a sea battle. This picture, although
excellent in many ways, does not show the hammocks that would
have been lashed to the lower part of the shrouds, nor the
boarding and damage nets that would have hung like huge
spiders' webs over the scene. The painting presents a tidy view
and omits the shattering damage caused by round shot to the
ships and men. Contemporary reports of major engagements refer
to huge jagged holes in the ships' sides, upturned and broken
guns, and decks running with blood.*

back cover: *This is a purely imaginative scene painted by
Nicholas Pocock, showing the five most important ships-of-the-
line in which Nelson served. The ships were in fact never seen
together in this way. From left to right the ships are* Agamemnon,
64 guns (built at Buckler's Hard), Captain, *74 guns,* Vanguard, *74
guns,* Elephant, *74 guns, and* Victory, *100 guns.*
H.M.S. Victory *was built in 1759 and so was an old ship by the
time of the Napoleonic Wars. She can still be seen today at
Portsmouth.*

title page: *Although not wearing uniforms in the modern sense
of the word these men would be instantly recognised by their
countrymen as seamen. They are wearing short jackets, long
trousers, and neckerchiefs and the seated sailor has a popular
seaman's hat, called a Monmouth hat; around his waist is an
apron made of leather or sailcloth. The pigtail was still popular,
though not regulation in 1806 when this etching was made.*

Contents

1 THE ADMIRALTY

For twenty-two years of war, with only one short interval of peace, Britain faced a formidable and efficient enemy whose armies, apparently invincible, marched where they wished on the mainland of Europe. These were the years of the French Revolutionary and Napoleonic Wars from 1793 to 1815.

French troops, led by intelligent and brave officers, defeated and subdued many countries which then had to provide more men and supplies to help the French. There were times when Britain stood alone against an enemy who commanded over a million trained and well-led soldiers. Britain, whose total population in 1801 was only about 10 million, could not have resisted long if that army had managed to cross the English Channel. The British fleet had to ensure that it never did.

The task of organising the British Navy and planning it actions fell to a small group of men who were directly res ponsible to the Government. Their full title was 'Lord Commissioners for executing the office of Lord High Admira of Great Britain' but they were usually called the 'Lords of th Admiralty', or 'Their Lordships' by those who served unde them. Their chairman was the First Lord but they were no necessarily peers in their own right and when not on duty Lord of the Admiralty may well have been a 'Sir' or a 'Mr'.

Sitting at a long table in a room in the Admiralty buildings i London this committee, sometimes only a small group of five o six, discussed and planned actions that would affect men an ships thousands of miles away. This was the central control o the whole Royal Navy and, while their secretaries made page of notes, these men laid down regulations and rules affectin everyday matters such as the price to be paid for a barrel o biscuits or vitally important ones like the complex manoeuvrin procedures for large battle fleets. Theirs was the complet control, but theirs also was the complete responsibility. If th Admiralty failed, Britain was lost.

The Navy Board and the Board of Ordnance

The Admiralty planned how war at sea was to be fought an issued orders direct to fleets and individual ships. They als appointed officers and authorised promotions. For most othe work Their Lordships had to have subcommittees to carry ou the details of their general policies. There were two mai committees which were responsible to the Admiralty an worked closely with them. These were the Navy Board and th Board of Ordnance.

The Board of Ordnance was responsible for supplying a weapons for the Navy, from small hand pistols to 68-pounde (31 kg) carronades. They controlled factories that manufac tured powder and guns, they employed transport to carry th munitions, and they contracted out work to civilian firms. The constantly experimented with new guns and powders an studied the effectiveness of existing weapons. As well a maintaining supplies, the Board of Ordnance was responsibl for equipment already in use. Every ship's captain had t account for every weapon on his ship and for the amount o shot and powder used. Guns and powder captured from th enemy had to be itemised and the lists sent to London.

The Admiralty Board room, where Their Lordships sat in conference. The large dial on the far wall was connected to a wind vane on the roof in order to have the wind direction, so vital for fleet movements in the Channel, constantly in view.

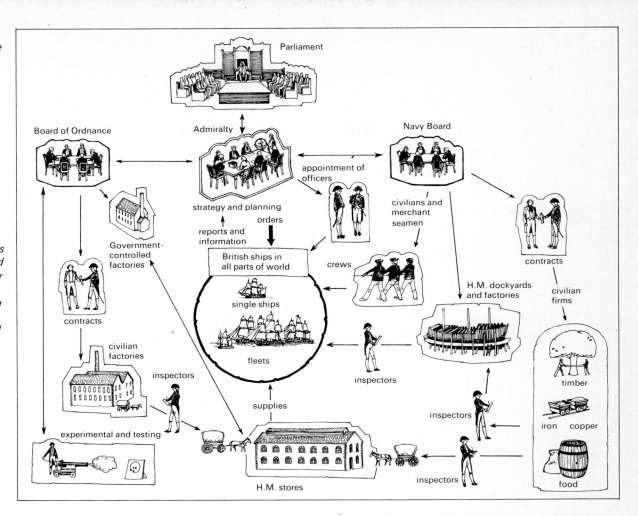

The diagram shows the main links in the chain of Admiralty control. Inspectors at various points were a method of curbing bribery, thieving and overpricing. They also checked the quality of goods received from civilian sources. Many timber merchants complained bitterly about the inspectors and said they would rather sell at a lower price than have the inspectors counting and checking the quality of each load of timber they delivered.

Parliament

Board of Ordnance

Admiralty

Navy Board

appointment of officers

strategy and planning

civilians and merchant seamen

reports and information

orders

contracts

Government-controlled factories

British ships in all parts of world

crews

contracts

civilian firms

single ships

H.M. dockyards and factories

civilian factories

inspectors

fleets

inspectors

timber

experimental and testing

supplies

inspectors

iron copper

inspectors

food

H.M. stores

Such an organisation could not function without a great number of officials and clerks, and the Board's offices contained hundreds of boxes and pigeon holes containing lists and letters dealing with every piece of ordnance in the Royal Navy. It was efficient and methodical. Woe betide any captain who could not produce records to account for all the powder and shot used during a firing practice at sea. A letter of reprimand would follow him even into the Pacific Ocean.

The Navy Board was responsible to the Admiralty for producing and delivering all the other requirements of the Navy. They had to ensure that ships were built, repaired and supplied with stores and equipment. They had direct control over all Government shipyards. Since much of their work had to be contracted out to civilian firms and they also employed civilian labour, the Navy Board was often referred to as the civil branch of the Navy. One of its most important functions was to ensure that the ships were manned, and they had the unpopular task of finding crews for the ever-growing fleets, and, even harder, ensuring that wages were paid.

Just like the Board of Ordnance the Navy Board had a highly complex structure with hundreds of inspectors, officials, clerks, and thousands of letters, contracts, lists and reports.

left: *The invasion of Britain was a real threat, not an illusion. In this picture, painted in 1804, Napoleon visits his troops and the invasion fleet gathered at Boulogne, just over 30 miles (48 kilometres) from Dover.*

opposite: *By careful planning and positioning of their ships, the Admiralty was able to protect British colonies and to guard the merchant ships that traded with them. The most valuable trade links were those with India and the West Indies. At the same time British warships roamed the world's oceans cutting the supply lines between enemy European countries and their colonies. Important enemy ports and islands were attacked, some were captured and garrisoned with British troops.*

The main tasks

As the long war continued the problems that faced the Admiralty naturally changed and so of course did the Admiralty's policies for. dealing with them. However, for most of the time certain basic problems existed that did not change:

1. THE THREAT OF INVASION. Because Britain was a group of small islands close to a hostile continent the landing of troops anywhere around her coasts was a possibility. Attempts by the revolutionaries to make landings in Scotland, Wales and Ireland had failed and the French abandoned any plan involving long voyages where adverse weather and the British fleet could so easily disrupt them. Even if successful, such landings would have been far away from supplies and reinforcements.

The key to invasion was the English Channel. It was only a few miles wide and under certain conditions even unseaworthy barges could cross. Given only a few hours of fine weather, thousands of crack French infantry could be storming the southern beaches of Britain. When Napoleon was at the height of his power there was an army of 200,000 on the north coast of France and a flotilla of invasion barges was being constructed.

The problem for the Admiralty was to ensure that at *all times* the British Navy had full control of the Channel waters.

2. THE THREAT TO COMMERCE. Britain's wealth and power relied heavily on her trade with Europe and numerous colonies throughout the world. The French control of Europe effectively cut Britain's continental trade, and her lifeline became the sea-routes to the rest of the world. If France could cut this lifeline using its sea-power, then Britain would be strangled by bankruptcy and poverty.

Lightly armed coastal traders were easy targets for even the smallest of French warships and privateers. If they were captured, vital coastal trade was disrupted and the enemy had even more small craft to ferry soldiers. This was a very important consideration for the Admiralty in the early years of the war, for it was only just over ten years since the American raider John Paul Jones had shown that a single determined captain could cause havoc around the British coast.

The more heavily armed deep-sea merchantmen could often defend themselves against smaller attackers but were no match for a French frigate or large privateer. If enemy warships had

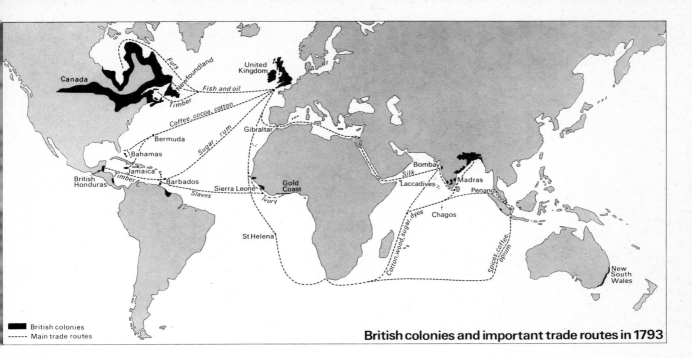

British colonies
Main trade routes

British colonies and important trade routes in 1793

Map labels: Canada, Furs, Newfoundland, Fish and oil, Timber, United Kingdom, Coffee, cocoa, cotton, Bermuda, Sugar, rum, Gibraltar, Bahamas, Jamaica, Timber, British Honduras, Barbados, Sierra Leone, Slaves, Ivory, Gold Coast, St Helena, Silk, Bombay, Laccadives, Madras, Penang, Cotton, wood, sugar, dyes, Chagos, Spices, coffee, opium, New South Wales

the freedom of the seas then Britain's trade, so vital to her existence, would suffer.

The task of the Admiralty was clear – to protect all British merchant ships wherever they might be.

3. COMBINED OPERATIONS. The first two tasks were defensive, but the only way of finally defeating France was by attack, usually with allies, but sometimes alone. Since the power of France lay in her apparently invincible armies this meant that British troops, with any possible allies, would have to come face to face with French troops.

Any ship of His Britannic Majesty's fleet was expected to be capable of mounting a small landing party using its own men and resources, but whole fleets had to be capable of giving full and effective support to military operations ashore. Supporting an army was a highly complex procedure. Previous wars had provided some experience of combined operations between the Army and the Navy; but there had been times when all had not gone well, and the relationship between the two forces was sometimes spoilt by misunderstanding and rivalry. However, if any large military actions were to be carried out on the main-

land of Europe or in the colonies, then the Admiralty would have to be ready to provide means of transport and support.

Barring the unexpected, these three tasks moulded all the plans of the Admiralty. The tasks were simple to state but enormously complicated to carry out. No Navy has ever had sufficient men or ships to be sure of performing such tasks satisfactorily. The Admiralty had to plan, manoeuvre and bluff as if engaged in a world-wide game of chess.

The problem of communication

In order to plan their moves and countermoves the Admiralty needed a continuous stream of information, not only about enemy movements, but also about the position and actions of their own ships. Little could be done to reduce the time-lag of months from ships in the Pacific and Indian Oceans but a way was found to speed up news arriving in Home Waters. Telegraphs were built which carried the news from Plymouth to Admiralty Building in London in twenty-four minutes instead of twenty-four hours.

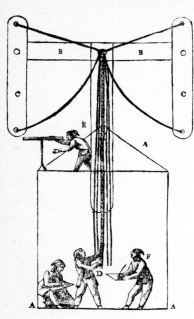

left: *The French aerial telegraph was built by Claude Chappé in 1794. There were 116 signal stations linking Paris with Lyons. (This was later extended to all main coastal regions.) Hourly information on any British ship in sight of the coast was transmitted to Paris.*

right: *A page from Popham's 'Telegraphic Signals or Marine Vocabulary'.*

below: *A British aerial telegraph system, based on the invention of the Reverend Murray, was in use in 1796 from ports on the south coast to London and back. The six holes in the board could be opened or closed in a variety of combinations to transmit coded messages.*

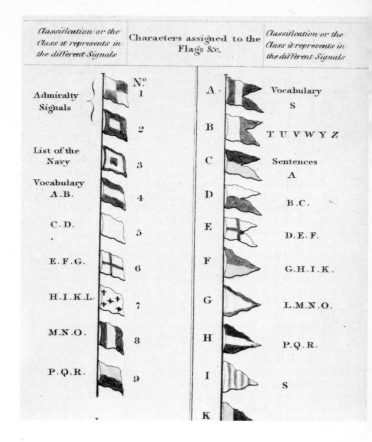

Classification or the Class it represents in the different Signals		Characters assigned to the Flags &c.		Classification or the Class it represents in the different Signals
Admiralty Signals	N.º 1		A	Vocabulary S
	2		B	T U V W Y Z
List of the Navy	3		C	Sentences A
Vocabulary A.B.	4		D	B.C.
C.D.	5		E	D.E.F.
E.F.G.	6		F	G.H.I.K.
H.I.K.L.	7		G	L.M.N.O.
M.N.O.	8		H	P.Q.R.
P.Q.R.	9		I	S
			K	

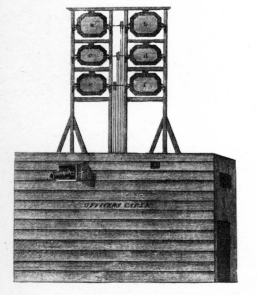

In the early years of the war the only means of communication from ship to ship was by using ten flags, numbered 0 to 9 which could be combined to give a numerical identification of any passage in the Signal Book. Admiral Howe had issued an improved Signal Book in 1776 and another in 1782. In 1790 he produced his own Signal Book which used this ten-flag system. In 1803 Popham's new code book, *Telegraphic Signals or Marine Vocabulary*, was issued to all ships and this enabled ships to send messages in language or code by a series of flags. Ships could now signal complicated messages quickly and clearly to other ships or to shore stations.

The telegraph and the new flag code book, backed up by the use of small fast sloops and pinnaces, cut down the time-lag and solved many of the problems of communication between Their Lordships and their ships-of-war. However, since the French had a similar efficient system, it did not give the Admiralty any great advantage over their enemy.

The main strategic principles

When the war began in 1793 the Admiralty controlled about 137 operational ships-of-the-line, and the French had about 90 with new ships being completed every month. As the war progressed the Dutch and Danish fleets passed into French hands. Then the greatest blow to the Admiralty came as the large Spanish fleet of 76 ships was added to the French total. Now every single British ship would have to be stationed with great care and used to its full advantage.

KEEPING OVERSEAS TRADE MOVING. The strategy for defending British bases and merchant ships abroad was basically a defensive one. Only occasionally were squadrons of French warships operating in the West or East Indies, so the Admiralty tended to send small groups of warships there with reliable and intelligent captains on a 'seek and destroy' commission.

The French, at little cost to themselves, had armed hundreds of small merchantmen as privateers and these ships roamed the seas looking for isolated British merchantmen. The Admiralty's answer was to re-establish the old convoy system for merchant ships with two or three frigates, and sometimes a '74', acting as guardians. Although there were occasional losses the convoy system proved very effective.

EUROPEAN STRATEGY. In European waters and ports the main battle fleets of the conflicting powers prepared for the fray to come. The Admiralty had to consider the threat of invasion, how to destroy the enemy fleets, and how to conserve its own strength against the heavy odds. Time was in the enemy's favour for, with ample supplies of European timber, its fleet grew in strength week by week, whereas Britain's supply of oak from Europe had been cut off by the French.

In 1793 the Admiralty acted quickly with a master strategy that turned out to be the most important decision of the war. All available warships put to sea and ringed Europe in a blockade. The word blockade may give the wrong impression, although one of its aims certainly was to cut Europe off from supplies and materials from other sources. It was also intended to keep the enemy fleets in separate ports, to catch them when

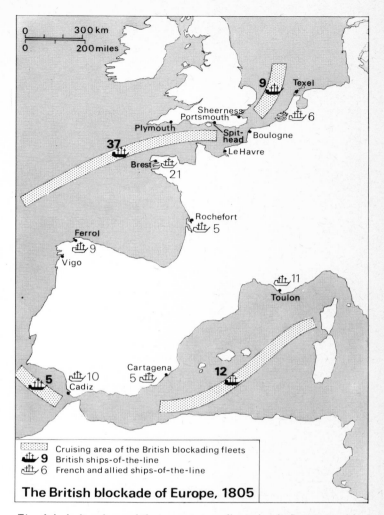

Cruising area of the British blockading fleets
9 British ships-of-the-line
6 French and allied ships-of-the-line

The British blockade of Europe, 1805

The Admiralty planned that any enemy fleet clearing port would be reported by frigates stationed near the port and met by a superior force of British ships-of-the-line before it could join other enemy fleets. The ports shown were the main ones used for equipping, refitting and sheltering the fleets.

they put to sea and to destroy them. It was a 'fighting blockade' which was maintained all year round. However, since the French had no intention of coming out to fight against superior numbers, the blockade was to drag on for twenty-two years.

2 THE MATERIAL

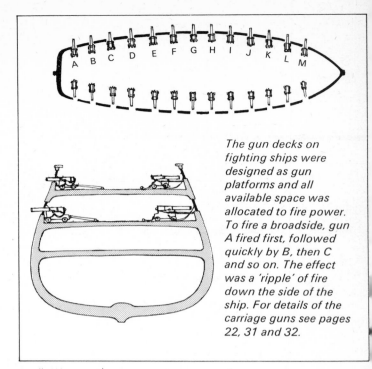

Their Lordships had to face the pressing problem of increasing their sea-force to counterbalance the massive sea-power of the enemy. Ships-of-war had to be built, guns, powder, shot and stores had to be supplied. Then men had to be found and trained as crew. The nation's funds and resources were poured into a massive effort to produce as many as possible of the most complex and powerful fighting machines of the day – warships.

The ordnance

The hitting power of a warship lay in its great guns. The design of a ship, the number of its crew and their positions were all contrived so that the guns could be used to their greatest effect. The Board of Ordnance had the responsibility of supplying the best possible guns, powder and shot, and throughout the country government factories and civilian firms under contract started work on producing the ordnance for the new ships.

All the guns were muzzle-loaders so had to be rolled inboard for loading. They were classified by the size of shot they could fire. The guns of the fleets consisted of five types of carriage guns; 6-pounders (firing a 6-pound shot – approximately 2.7 kg), 12-pounders (5.5 kg), 18-pounders (8.2 kg), 24-pounders (10.9 kg) and 32-pounders (14.5 kg). To maintain the ship's stability the heaviest guns were placed on the lower decks and the lightest on the upper deck. They had to be on carriages so that the powerful recoil could be absorbed by the gun rolling back under the control of breech ropes and tackles.

Ships-of-the-line carried the most guns. A first-rate presented three tiers of nearly fifty guns each side and could throw a broadside weight of about 2,500 pounds (1,135 kg) of metal an effective distance of one and a half miles (2.4 km). Ashore some 42-pounders (19 kg) and 32-pounders (14.5 kg) were installed in permanent fortresses but the largest land armies rarely used anything heavier than a 12-pounder (5.5 kg); all the French

The gun decks on fighting ships were designed as gun platforms and all available space was allocated to fire power. To fire a broadside, gun A fired first, followed quickly by B, then C and so on. The effect was a 'ripple' of fire down the side of the ship. For details of the carriage guns see pages 22, 31 and 32.

artillery at the battle of Waterloo (286 guns) could not match a 100-gun warship firing half its guns. Descriptions by eye-witnesses tell of the wind from a broadside flattening the waves and taking the wind from the sails of nearby ships. Because of excessive recoil and the danger of damaging the ship, all the guns were never fired at once in practice and only rarely in battle. Firing a broadside usually meant using all the guns from one side of the ship, but not necessarily firing them all at once.

Although slow and ponderous a ship-of-the-line was a floating fortress with a terrible fire-power that could destroy towns as well as ships.

The carronade

A short-barrelled carronade or 'smasher' was in general use after 1779 but such guns were never counted in the rating of British ships. The number of carronades carried by a ship-of-the-line varied but it was common to have three or four on the forecastle. They were of no use at ranges over 500 yards (455

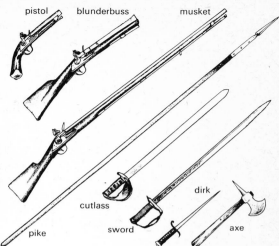

above: *Small Arms. Hand weapons of various types were placed in racks beside the guns and at other convenient spots, such as around the base of a mast, so they were ready for use by boarding parties or to repel boarders.*

above: *The port carronade of the forecastle of H.M.S.* Victory. *Unlike the other guns, the carronade recoiled by sliding back with its wooden base. The lower wooden base did not move on recoil but was pivoted at the ship's side and the inboard end had wheels to enable it to slew (swing) left or right.*

right: *Types of Shot. The standard missile was the iron round shot, or cannonball. For cutting rigging, sails, and spars one of the various chain shots was used. Heated shot was intended to burn a ship's timbers when it struck home; but it was dangerous to use since it had to be made red hot and the wad between the hot shot and the powder cartridge had to be made of green wood, wrapped with rope yarns. It was normally fired only from coastal forts against attacking ships. Grapeshot spread small iron balls and was used both to clear enemy decks of men and to cut rigging.*

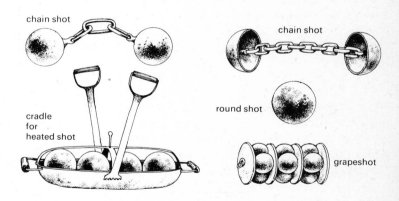

metres) but were extremely effective at very close range since the biggest could throw a massive 68-pound (30.8-kg) cannonball or a murderous hail of hundreds of musket-balls.

Classes of fighting ship

Different classes of warship were built for different purposes. Even among ships-of-the-line the difference in draught (depth from the waterline down to the keel) enabled the smaller fourth-rates to enter harbours where a first-rate would have run aground, and, usually, the larger the ship, the slower she sailed. For immediate recognition of a ship's capabilities they were given a general classification and a more specific 'rating'. Given a ship's rating, an experienced seaman would know how much rigging, the size and number of anchors, the number of guns, the amount of stores, and the crew that she carried.

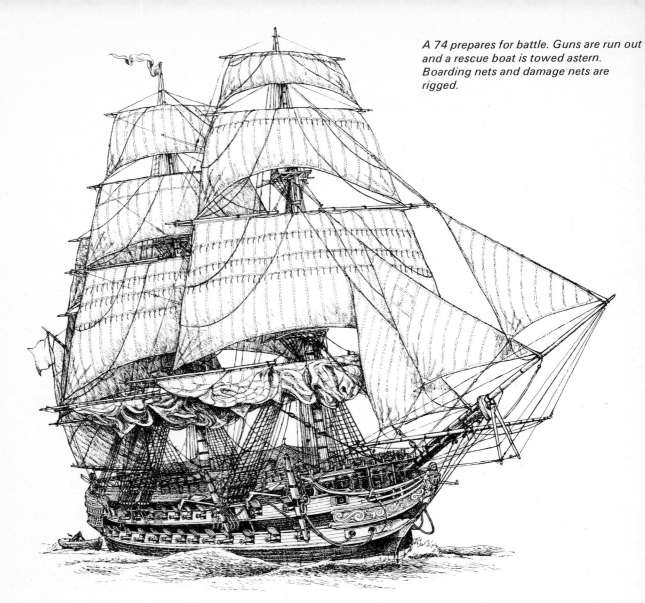

A 74 prepares for battle. Guns are run out and a rescue boat is towed astern. Boarding nets and damage nets are rigged.

THE GREAT FIGHTING MACHINE – THE 74. The knowledge and experience gained in the early years of the war perfected the most versatile and popular ship-of-the-line – the third-rate with 74 guns. Sailing and manoeuvring with a delicacy and speed that enabled it to act alone or with a group of frigates, yet powerful and solid enough to stand in a battle line, the 74 was popular with seamen, officers and Their Lordships. Every inch of the 74 was a product of war experience; she was a fighting machine and a floating fortress, designed to carry her great guns in all weathers to all parts of the world. The Fighting 74 was the backbone of the Navy that beat Napoleon.

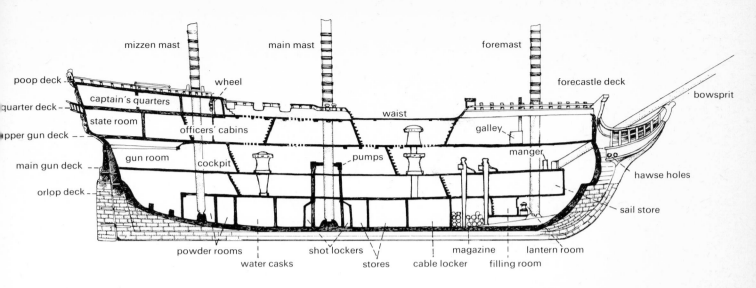

mizzen mast   main mast   foremast

poop deck

wheel   forecastle deck

quarter deck

captain's quarters

bowsprit

state room

waist

officers' cabins

galley

upper gun deck

manger

main gun deck

gun room   cockpit   pumps

hawse holes

orlop deck

sail store

powder rooms   shot lockers   magazine   lantern room

water casks   stores   cable locker   filling room

above: *A simplified section of a 74.
There were two gun decks, carrying
most of the guns (which are not
shown in this diagram), and above
these were the forecastle and quarter
deck and finally the poop. There were
variations in the design of 74s,
especially in the layout below the
orlop deck. In many 74s the waist was
crossed with heavy beams and the
ship's boats were stored there (as
shown on the front cover picture).*

right: *On the quarter deck looking aft
towards the poop deck. Although
taken on H.M.S.* Victory, *a three
decker, the view on a 74 would be
similar. Behind the hammock nettings,
on the poop deck, top right, is the base
of the mizzen mast. The row of buckets
would have held sand. Below the
poop deck is the wheel and binnacle.
More hammock nettings can be seen
on the ship's side where the ladder
leads up to the poop. On a 74 the
doors lead along a passage to the
Captain's quarters.*

Classes of British fighting ships in 1800

RATING	COST WITHOUT GUNS	NUMBER OF GUNS	WEIGHT OF BROADSIDE lb (kg)	NUMBER OF CREW	LENGTH OF MAIN GUN DECK ft (m)	NUMBER IN COMMISSION IN 1800	THROUGH DECKS
Ships-of-the-line Considered to be of sufficient strength to form part of a battle fleet							
First-rate	£100,000	100-120	2,500 (1,134)	850-950	180 (55)	11	3
Second-rate	£60,000	90 or 98	2,300 (1,043)	740-750	170-180 (52-55)	21	3
Third-rate	£50,000	64. 74 or 80	1,764 (800)	640-720	160-170 (49-52)	148	2
Fourth-rate	£24,000	50	800 (363)	350	150 (46)	20	2
Frigates Much faster with better sailing qualities than ships-of-the-line; excellent for independent work but not capable of forming a line of battle							
Fifth-rate	£20,000	32, 36, 38, 40 or 44	636-350 (288-159)	215-320	130-150 (40-46)	162	1
Sixth-rate	£13,000	20, 24 or 28	250-180 (113-82)	160-200	120-130 (37-40)	51	1
Sloops and pinnaces Very fast; used for river and inshore work and for carrying messages							
No rating	about £9,000	18	54 (25)	115	90-110 (27-34)	134	1
Bomb vessels Specially strengthened vessels, carrying a mortar for shore bombardment							
No rating	varied	8	24 (11)	varied	100 (30)	127	1
Transports Slow; usually old merchantmen converted to carry horses, troops or supplies.							
No rating	varied	varied		varied		114	varied

The guns itemised in the table are carriage guns, not carronades (see page 10).

Note how many types of ship were in commission in 1800. Among the ships-of-the-line it is obvious that the Admiralty found third-rates of special value. These were the famous Fighting 74s (see page 12). The big frigate, the fifth-rate, is also present in large numbers which indicates the value placed on it. The importance of constant communication is emphasised by the large number of message-carrying sloops and pinnaces. The Navy's readiness to attack land bases in force is shown by the number of bomb vessels.

Dockyards and stores

In the rivers and harbours of Britain, shipbuilders worked to supply the demands of the Admiralty, for in wartime the naval dockyards alone could not build nearly enough ships. Buckler's Hard on the River Beaulieu near Southampton was a typical civilian dockyard building warships under contract to the Navy Board. Employing only about forty men (and all timber was moved on carts or sledges) this shipyard built a long list of excellent ships.

Since Buckler's Hard was a civilian yard there would have been no ordnance or supply stores there. Once launched a ship was towed to the naval yard at Portsmouth and fitted with her guns there by the Board of Ordnance, and all her other supplies by the Navy Board.

A photograph of a model of Buckler's Hard as it may have appeared during the Napoleonic Wars. The main layout is still recognisable today.

1 The rough timber yard, where local timber, brought in carts, awaited the sawyers. It was sorted and stacked into piles of similar curvature.
2 The jetty where imported timber was landed and stacked.
3 The main street where the sawn timber was stacked and allowed to season before being selected for ship building.
4 The shipbuilders' homes.
5 The master builder's home.
6 Euryalus, a 36-gun frigate, and Swiftsure, a 74, under construction.

Ships built at Buckler's Hard

	RATING	LAUNCHED		RATING	LAUNCHED
Santa Margarita	36-gun frigate	1793	*Swiftsure*	74-gun third-rate	1804
Cerberus	32-gun frigate	1794	*Crowler*	16 guns	1804
Bittern	16 guns	1796	*Fervent*	16 guns	1805
Boadicea	38-gun frigate	1797	*Dexterous*	16 guns	1805
Snake	16 guns	1797	*Columbine*	16 guns	1806
Abundance	24-gun frigate	1799	*Hussar*	38-gun frigate	1807
Spencer	74-gun third-rate	1800	*Victorious*	74-gun third-rate	1808
L'Aigle	36-gun frigate	1801	*Hannibal III*	74-gun third-rate	1810
Starling	16 guns	1802	*Medina*	18-gun sloop	1813
Snipe	16 guns	1802	*Carron*	18-gun sloop	1813
Vixen	16 guns	1802	*Tay*	20-gun frigate	1813
Euryalus	36-gun frigate	1803	*Fowey*	20-gun frigate	1814

These were the ships built on the stocks but the Admiralty sometimes added more guns and so altered the classification. For example, *Medina* and *Carron* were given 20 guns each and were classified as frigates. During the same period 12 merchant ships were also built.

3 THE OFFICERS

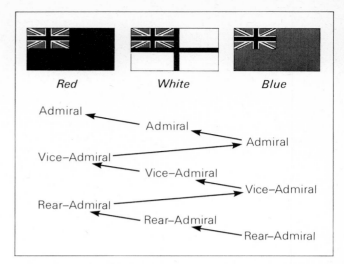

Red   White   Blue

Admiral ← Admiral ← Admiral

Vice–Admiral ← Vice–Admiral ← Vice–Admiral

Rear–Admiral ← Rear–Admiral ← Rear–Admiral

Seniority of admirals was based on the old three-squadron system (the Red, White and Blue Squadrons). Each squadron was traditionally commanded by an admiral. The admiral commanded the centre ships in the squadron, the vice-admiral those in the lead and the rear-admiral commanded the ships in the rear.

Commanding officers

With the Board of Ordnance and the Navy Board providing the ships and their guns, the next crucial task for the Admiralty was to decide who would *use* these ships, who was to command in their name? The promotion system of the Navy provided them with a group of men who could link them directly to the constantly moving fleets; these were the admirals.

ADMIRAL. Promoted automatically by seniority from the rank of captain, the admirals were all experienced men who had started their life at sea as midshipmen. They had proved their seamanship and fighting qualities, but knowledge and spirit were not always enough to commend them to Their Lordships. The Admiralty needed men whom they could take into their confidence, men who could understand their overall strategy and men who could be trusted to carry out their policies with intelligence and single-mindedness. Unlike the other seagoing ship's officers the admirals were almost sure to have met Their Lordships and talked for long hours with them in Admiralty House. The Admiralty had to know their admirals personally before entrusting them with direct responsibility, and, once they knew them, they could allocate tasks suitable to the capabilities of each man. Some men were better suited to administration ashore, some were given command of shore establishments, others were appointed as governors of British colonies. Since admirals held their rank for life the Admiralty had to find tasks for some very old men, or else talk them into voluntary retirement. Finally, they decided upon the admirals who would be in command of the ships at sea.

Selecting the best men for the job was made easier by having a large number to choose from. Once there had been only nine admirals but by 1807 there were 166 flag-officers (admirals flew their own flags and were often referred to as flag-officers).

In each fleet, the lowest ranking flag-officer was Rear-Admiral of the Blue and the highest was Admiral of the Red.

The Admiral of the Red was known as the Admiral of the Fleet. His salary was about £1,900; rear-admirals received about £800 a year. Nelson was made Rear-Admiral of the Blue in 1797, Rear-Admiral of the Red in 1799, and in 1801 he was Vice-Admiral of the White. At Trafalgar he was flying the White Ensign which was later adopted as the only Royal Navy Ensign, the Red Ensign being adopted by the Merchant Navy.

A seagoing admiral controlled a large number of ships but he did not command a ship in the same way that a captain did. Instead, an admiral chose a suitable ship from amongst his fleet and this became his flagship; his admiral's flag was flown from this ship when he was aboard. He could change his mind at any time and move his flag to another ship. A large first-rate had plenty of space to provide a great cabin for the benefit of an admiral, but on most other types of ship the unfortunate captain of the vessel chosen had to abandon his living quarters to the admiral and his staff.

Worse still, he had to handle his ship and control his men under the stern eye of his superior officer. Life for officers and men on a ship chosen as flagship was uncomfortable and tense.

POST-CAPTAIN. Although it was not a title of rank it was, and still is, common practice to call any officer in complete charge of a ship 'Captain'. A Lieutenant Jones, for example, in command of a small sloop *Ariel*, would be called 'Captain Jones' by his crew and port officials. He would be called 'Lieutenant Jones, Captain of the sloop *Ariel*' by his fellow officers but the Admiralty would be likely to address him as 'Lieutenant Jones, Commander of the sloop *Ariel*'. The actual *rank* of captain was obtained when the Admiralty promoted an officer to be a post-captain.

Once appointed by merit of his past experience and capabilities, any officer who became a post-captain was settled on a guaranteed path. He was firmly placed in the seniority list, which meant that no one could be 'jumped' over him in promotion and that he moved up the list as senior officers above him either died or left the service. If he lived long enough and did not disgrace himself, he could become Admiral of the Fleet simply by waiting his turn.

With all doubts about his future removed the captain could expect command of a small frigate at least, then perhaps a fifth-rate and so on until he commanded a first-rate. From time to time he could be given command of a small squadron of ships and carry the temporary title of commodore. Post-captains commanded almost all of the fighting ships of the Navy and it was on these men that the Admiralty heavily relied for carrying out instructions with common sense and initiative.

A captain was responsible to his admiral, or to the Admiralty, if acting alone, for the condition of his ship, guns, stores, the conduct of his crew and officers, and their fighting efficiency. In battle he was expected to fulfil his general orders regardless of any risk to his life and also to use his initiative if circumstances changed. Since the captain held full responsibility he was given absolute control over his men.

In accord with the regulations laid down by Their Lordships a captain held the power of life and death over his officers and men. He was, therefore, a powerful and feared figure aboard his ship. No seaman or officer spoke to him unless on ship's business and they cleared the starboard side of the quarter deck whenever he came from his cabin and did not approach him unless he called them. Guarded by an armed marine at the door of his stateroom, the captain lived an isolated life in his well-appointed accommodation.

The following pictures by T. Rowlandson, dated 1799, show naval officers in full dress uniform. See the front cover for the colouring of the uniforms.

above left: *POST-CAPTAIN His salary varied according to the size of ship he commanded. On a first-rate he would earn £32 4s 0d per lunar month and on a sixth-rate £16 16s 0d.*

above right: *MIDSHIPMAN This is how a midshipman would have wished to appear. Some youngsters with wealthy parents may have dressed like this but midshipmen usually wore top hats, frock coats and long trousers.*

Commissioned officers

MIDSHIPMAN. With only a few exceptions, all the officers of His Britannic Majesty's fleets came from middle- or upper-class families. They were usually sons of country squires or naval officers. The only method of becoming an officer in the Navy was by patronage. This meant that someone in the boy's family or a close friend of the family had to know a serving captain well enough to ask him to take the youngster aboard his ship. Once accepted, usually about the age of 11 or 12, he joined the ship as captain's servant and awaited the first vacancy as a midshipman. Once appointed as midshipman he was paid £1 13s 6d per lunar month and after two years service he could receive £2 15s 6d in a first-rate or £2 0s 6d in a sixth-rate.

There was a six-year minimum sea-service requirement before he could sit his lieutenant's oral examination and two years of this service had to be as a midshipman. During this time the boy studied navigation, seamanship, shiphandling and sea-warfare and received certificates of conduct and 'officer-like qualities' from the captain. The number of midshipmen carried varied from twenty-four in a first-rate to three or four in a small frigate. At battle stations they assisted the lieutenants and captain, acting as messengers and signalmen, and helping with the great guns; experienced 'middys' could have charge of up to six guns.

Once his sea-service had been completed, the midshipman had to await the captain's pleasure for his promotion. Although only the Crown, via the Admiralty, could grant commissions, it was up to the captain to present candidates. There was no other way to become a lieutenant. A midshipman who was not presented as a candidate for the examinations by his captain could make no official complaint, he could only wait, and hope.

SUB-LIEUTENANT. This was a posting not a rank. It was taken by officers who had passed their lieutenant's examinations but had not yet received Their Lordship's commission and so were really awaiting promotion. A sub-lieutenant was a purely temporary post.

LIEUTENANT. This was the first fully commissioned rank for naval officers but further promotion was not guaranteed and some men remained lieutenants all their sea-going careers. Promotion from lieutenant depended on luck, patronage, and ability. It was possible for intelligent and capable seamen to become lieutenants, but without social connections with senior naval officers they could rise no further.

The chances for an ambitious lieutenant were varied. He could become a junior lieutenant on a flagship and work under the direction of the admiral. A ship-of-the-line carried nine lieutenants and he could work his way up to the position of first lieutenant, which meant he was second in command to the captain. If he proved his worth, was in the right place at the right time, and some senior officer remembered his name, he

left: *LIEUTENANT When in view of influential senior officers a lieutenant would always strive to dress like this. On fifth- or sixth-rates he would probably only wear full uniform on special occasions.*

right: *PURSER His dress was unimportant and he often wore civilian clothes.*

far right: *CAPTAIN OF MARINES The highest paid of all the ship's officers – only the captain received more. He maintained a smart, military appearance, with the scarlet coat and crimson sash of an army officer.*

could be given command of a sloop or a bomb vessel, or temporary command of a prize ship. Since lieutenants were in charge of the various sections of the ship, such as the forecastle, main deck, gun decks and signals there were plenty of opportunities to show their mettle.

For an officer desirous of promotion the time spent as a lieutenant was a nerve-racking period. Since he was always striving to appear smart and officer-like, most of his pay went on uniforms and weapons. With the exception of first lieutenants on flagships, who received £9 2s, all other lieutenants were paid £8 8s per lunar month and when ashore awaiting a new ship they went on half pay. At any time a lieutenant could be dismissed or see luckier and younger men promoted over his head.

All the officers mentioned so far were either of commissioned rank or expecting to become commissioned officers. They all had the right to walk the quarter deck and use the wardroom. Between them and the crew existed a strict barrier of rank re-

SURGEON. The surgeon was in charge of the general health of the whole crew and his most important role was in battle when he took charge of the cockpit and attended to the wounded. Since amputations were carried out without anaesthetic he was unpopular with the crew and, like doctors ashore, was considered by the officers as a type of tradesman. He too had to supply his own instruments.

PURSER. He was the ship's 'shopkeeper' controlling all articles sold on board and taking a commission on each sale. He was in charge of the 'slops' (cheap ready-made or second-hand clothing) and issued dungaree, needles and thread for the sailors to make or mend clothes. At battle stations he helped in the distribution of powder. Since his position offered opportunities for deliberate falsifying of account books he had to pay Caution Money before taking up his post. He paid £1,200 on a first-rate, £1,000 on a second-rate, £800 on a third-rate and £600 on fourth- and fifth-rates. If found guilty of misconduct he was dismissed and lost his Caution Money.

CHAPLAIN. This post was not always filled, especially on small vessels. The chaplain was spiritual advisor to the whole crew and at battle stations he assisted the surgeon in the cockpit. Since, socially, the Church was a 'respectable' profession he was usually accepted by the commissioned officers as a 'gentleman'.

Marine officers

All marines had taken an oath of loyalty to the Crown and one of their functions was to maintain the established authority (usually the captain's), if that authority was acting according to the prescribed regulations. Their loyalty was never in question. As long as the marine officer knew that the captain was acting in the interests of the Crown, support was certain, even for shooting members of the crew who panicked during a battle. On the other hand the captain knew that marine officers would also arrest him if they received orders from a more senior officer.

All Navy ships carried a marine detachment and at least one officer. In first-rates there was a captain of marines and two lieutenants. Since marine officers held the King's commission they were socially on a par with the naval officers. During battle the marine officer was usually stationed on the poop with a dozen or more of his men.

enforced by social differences. There were however some positions of responsibility that placed the men who held them among the commissioned officers sharing their privileges, even though some of them were not considered to be in the same social class. These were the warrant-officers of wardroom rank who used the quarter deck, dined with the officers, and often gave them expert advice; but the authority of the commissioned rank was never in question.

Warrant-officers of wardroom rank

THE MASTER. The master was an expert navigator holding his post by his proven ability to navigate with accuracy and safety. He usually carried his own charts, books, sextant and other instruments, and could offer advice to the captain, but could not insist on his advice being followed. Most masters were captains from merchant ships who had volunteered for Royal Navy service and had satisfied the Admiralty as to their capabilities in navigation and ship management.

4 THE RATINGS

The following is a made up, but typical, description of how a new ship may have taken on its crew, housed them, trained them, and controlled them. We must imagine a battleship at anchor in a British harbour. It is fully equipped and fitted out, it only awaits its crew.

The crew comes aboard

Each of the ship's officers has been appointed by the Admiralty and all have received letters instructing them to proceed to the port where their ship lies and to contact the first lieutenant and report for duty. They take up lodgings at the inn nearest the harbour and find that the first lieutenant has already been there for a week. He has been inspecting the ship and meeting the first batch of men sent by the Navy Board. This first group turns out to be the warrant-officers, that is the boatswain, the carpenter and the gunner, along with a group of experienced and reliable men transferred from other ships, most of them able seamen. These men will form a well-trained and disciplined core. Around them will be moulded the rest of the crew which is bound to be quota men, pressed men and volunteers, most of them inexperienced in the ways of the sea, and of the Navy in particular.

VOLUNTEERS. The next day brings news of a riotous gang of drunken men who are spending money fast and causing a great disturbance in the town. The lieutenant now knows that his volunteers have arrived and he sends his officers to tour the inns and jails to collect them.

These volunteers are men who have joined the Navy willingly and received a bounty for doing so, usually about £5. They are young men without a job, with a blind love of the sea or a desire for adventure; or else older men who knew they could not have escaped the press-gang and decided that if they were to end in the Navy in any case they might as well have the bounty money.

Using a corner of the bar at the inn, the lieutenant and a committee of other officers and warrant-officers examine the volunteers for physical fitness and try to judge their potential as seamen. Anyone with experience of a trade that would help a warrant-officer is rated as an ordinary seaman, the rest are rated as landsmen.

QUOTA MEN. When the detachment of marines and their officers arrive the first lieutenant orders all officers and men to take up their quarters on board ship and to make it ready for sea. He is very conscious of the fact that he must present a neat and tidy ship to the new captain when he arrives. In the midst of all this work he is not pleased to hear that a party of quota men are on the quayside under armed guard. Under the Quota Act of 1795 county towns have to supply the Navy with a stipulated number of men. In theory this is a simple form of conscription but most towns simply clear their jails, round up vagrants and tramps and send them off under military guard. There is little chance of finding any promising material among them; however they still have to be listed, examined, and then deloused and washed.

The quota men are issued with hammocks and shown their quarters. From now on a ship's boat with marine sentries circles the ship in case some of the newcomers decide that they prefer life in jail to life at sea.

PRESSED MEN. At last the captain arrives, reads his commission to the assembled men, flies his long narrow pennant from the masthead, and inspects the ship. Since the ship is still below its full complement of men the captain issues a warrant for the lieutenant to impress civilians from the port area. For the rest of the week the officer, the boatswain and a party of trusted seamen move around the narrow streets and in taverns and lodging houses searching for any suitable man, fit enough to become a sailor. The impress party carry wooden cudgels in case of reluctant 'recruits' or opposition by their friends. Swords and firearms are not carried since a wounded or damaged 'recruit' is of no value.

The press-gang's methods are simple and quick. A candidate is spotted, approached and then marched smartly down to the quay where a ship's boat awaits. Only men with exemption papers showing that their occupation is necessary to the war effort are released, as are sailors on leave and soldiers. Unfortunately the word soon spreads that the press-gang is in operation and the streets are uncommonly deserted. Their last

Press-gang selecting men: cartoon by Collings, 1790.

victim is a man trying to evade them by dressing in women's clothes, but he is the last and, to the relief of the citizens, the gang retires to the ship.

MERCHANT SEAMEN. Although still undermanned the captain must now put to sea, but he still has a chance to make up his crew numbers. Cruising off the coast he waits for a homeward-bound merchantman. The ship is stopped, boarded and most of the crew impressed, leaving only sufficient men to sail her into port. This is lawful procedure but the merchant captain is unwilling to hand over his best seamen and men are found hiding in the holds and inside cargo bales.

Now with a more or less complete crew the captain has one final act to perform in order to obtain the best possible crew. He stops an outward-bound merchant ship. The naval captain cannot reduce the crew of an outward-bound vessel, but he can exchange crew members. Collecting all the weak, sick and mentally slow from the quota and pressed men he hands them over to the angry merchant captain and collects the same number from the best of the merchant crew.

Now that his vessel is fully manned, the captain continues on his way according to his written instructions while the warrant-officers and able seamen set about forming the newcomers into some form of fighting and sailing unit.

Quarters

The newcomers to ships and the sea find themselves in a bewildering world. When shown their new quarters they find no rooms or cabins, just the length of a gun deck with a low deckhead (ceiling) and rows of massive guns and equipment lining the sides. With the gun ports closed and a dim light coming from where the ladders ascend through hatchways it is like a dank shallow cellar. This, they are told, is likely to be their home for the next few years.

Groups of eight men are shown the space between two guns and told to make themselves comfortable. They find that a table can be lowered from the beams above and held suspended by a rope cradle. Benches serve as seats at the tables and racks on the ship's side hold mess utensils and have space for one small bag for each seaman. The purser's assistants supply each man with two hammocks, a straw mattress, knife, spoon, pot, bowl and platter. He is told to keep the knife on his person at all times, to stow the hammocks in the hammock nettings on deck and that he will have to pay for anything lost or broken. Stern warrant-officers threaten the new men with terrible punishments if the area is not kept spotlessly clean. Unshaven men are forcibly reminded that no one, not even an officer, goes unshaven in the Navy. For cold weather they are issued with a short loose coat of thick hessian and a tarred canvas apron. Any other clothing will have to be either what they are wearing or else purchased from the purser's 'slop chest' or from the sale of a dead man's effects. They are now one of the 'Jolly Tars of Old England' and there is no way out. Already they can sense the absolute power of the officers. Desertion is punishable by hanging and the marine sentries carry loaded muskets. They are trapped and can only try to make the best of it.

There are some consolations. They had dreaded the thought of 300 men slinging their hammocks from the beams; it would have meant that each hammock would be jammed up against its neighbours, but they find that normally only half of the men sleep at one time; the rest are out on watch. Men who have found themselves in a group of what appear to be unclean savages are relieved to hear that each month any man can ask to change to another group, and such requests are rarely refused.

Accepting the inevitable, many landsmen sleep deeply that first night, for the hammocks are far more comfortable than shore beds.

This photograph from H.M.S. Victory shows the tables lowered and benches in position. Two hammocks are shown but at night hundreds would have been slung beneath the beams.

'Saturday Night at Sea'. This drawing showing a mess group of sailors is dated about 1840 but little has changed over forty years. It gives an excellent impression of the variety of sailors' dress.

Food

The mainstay of the food supply was beer and biscuits. The beer was small beer and rotted in the cask after about twelve weeks. If it ran out, a cheap wine was substituted. The biscuits were baked in shore bakeries into hard 4 oz (113 gm) circles and were in plentiful supply. Extremely difficult to eat in their hard state, they could be softened by being left for a few days in damp air and then could be chewed, fried, or ground into crumbs that could be eaten with any meal.

The meat was salted in casks and after being kept for many

Approximate food allowance stipulated by the Admiralty for one man for one week

	BISCUITS lb (g)	BEER gal (l)	BEEF lb (g)	PORK lb (g)	PEASE pints (ml)	OATMEAL pints (ml)	SUGAR oz (g)	BUTTER oz (g)	CHEESE oz (g)
Sunday	1 (454)	1 (4½)		1 (454)	½ (286)				
Monday	1 (454)	1 (4½)				½ (286)	2 (57)	2 (57)	4 (114)
Tuesday	1 (454)	1 (4½)	2 (908)						
Wednesday	1 (454)	1 (4½)			½ (286)	½ (286)	2 (57)	2 (57)	4 (114)
Thursday	1 (454)	1 (4½)		1 (454)	½ (286)				
Friday	1 (454)	1 (4½)			½ (286)	½ (286)	2 (57)	2 (57)	2 (57)
Saturday	1 (454)	1 (4½)	2 (908)						

months, or even years, it was so hard that seamen found it could be carved and polished to make ornaments.

For breakfast there was oatmeal but most seamen preferred crushed biscuits in water. Dinner consisted of pea soup, meat or duffs (made from a mixture of flour, salt and beef fat). Supper was cheese, but due to the Admiralty's policy of 'oldest stores to be eaten first' it was often riddled with long red worms.

Newcomers to life at sea soon found that any items of edible food could be used as coins of the realm were used ashore. Again they found there were consolations. At noon each day the 'cook' from each group collected the grog allowance. For each man there was a quarter of a pint (142 ml) of pure rum diluted with three parts of water with lemon juice and sugar added. The same allowance was issued at suppertime.

The food allowances varied once a ship had been at sea for some time. Supplies inevitably ran out and if replacements were not found then substitutes were arranged such as tea, cocoa, vinegar, beans, rice, sugar lumps, and oil. Chewing tobacco or tarred oakum soaked in grog became very popular.

Jobs

As the warship with its mixed crew of experts and newcomers edged away from the coast, the officers and warrant-officers immediately set about training their crew into a unit that could sail the ship under all conditions. Each British fighting ship, regardless of size, had the same method of dividing its crew into working sections. Any seaman transferred to another ship would find the tasks and organisation exactly the same. A simplified picture of the organisation is given in the table under cruising (non-battle) conditions.

THE WATCH SYSTEM. Under normal cruising conditions alert and fresh seamen were needed for all of the twenty-four hours of the day so the majority of the crew were divided into two sections called the starboard and larboard watches. Each watch worked for four hours, relaxed or slept for the next four hours, and then started another four-hours' work. Watch systems could vary from ship to ship but this 'four on, four off' shared by two watches was the most common.

The organisation of a naval ship under cruising (non-battle) conditions

OFFICERS	CAPTAIN	
Quarter deck	*Commissioned officers* first lieutenant third lieutenant, etc second lieutenant midshipman	*Marine officers*
	Warrant-officers (wardroom rank) master purser chaplain surgeon	
CREW Before the mast (forward of the mainmast)	*Warrant-officers (not wardroom rank)* boatswain carpenter gunner	*Marine sergeants*
	Minor warrant-officers sailmaker caulker ropemaker cook armourer master-at-arms cooper	
	Assistants to warrant-officers	*Marines*
	Rest of crew split into sections and watches topmen afterguard forecastlemen waisters idlers	

The amount of work called for during the 'four hours on' depended on the type of work and the state of the weather. For example there were eight helmsmen on a watch on a first-rate but only four at a time were needed to work the huge double wheel so they took turns of two hours. In bad weather all eight would be called to stand their watch on deck beside the wheel.

In emergencies and foul weather conditions the watch system was abandoned and 'all hands' were called on deck to help out with the work.

IDLERS. To be called an idler was more of a compliment than an insult for it simply meant that this seaman's work did not fit into the watch system. It could be that the man who fed the captain's geese kept in the ship's boats was an idler, but the name could also apply to the master-at-arms, the armourer and the cooper.

TOPMEN. These were active, agile and reliable seamen who worked all the yards above the main yard on the fore, main and mizzen masts. Since they were always in full view of the ship's officers and passing ships they were expected to be smart and almost acrobatic in their actions.

FORECASTLEMEN. These were older and less-active seamen but usually of great experience and very reliable. Their duty was about the anchors, bowsprit and forecastle where they could be relied upon to carry out their duties without undue supervision. It was from amongst the forecastlemen that promotions were made to boatswain and gunner's mate.

AFTERGUARD. On the quarter deck, and the decks immediately below, the less able seamen and landsmen who were beginning to show promise worked under the eyes of the officers. The work, manning the mainsail braces and keeping the afterpart of the ship clean, was relatively easy, but the ambition of most of the afterguard was to become a forecastleman or a topman.

WAISTERS. In the middle, or waist, of the ship, directly under the eyes of the rest of the ship's crew, the least able, the least intelligent, and the trouble makers performed the heaviest and most unpleasant tasks. They handled the mainsheets, cleaned the pigstyes and manned the main pumps. To be called a waister was an insult and men tried to be transferred to the afterguard, not just because of the derogatory term and heavy work but because in battle the waist of the ship always suffered the heaviest damage and the highest casualties.

Ratings and pay

The men who found themselves, willingly or not, as part of the crew of a British man-of-war either quickly adapted to the conditions and work or were ruthlessly disciplined into a reluctant acceptance of their fate. If they resigned themselves to the almost God-like power of those in authority above them and showed themselves capable, they found a variety of tasks and promotions open to them. We have just seen the general division of the crew into watches and idlers and into the grades of topmen, forecastlemen, waisters and afterguard. Now we will look more closely at the ratings and the tasks available to the seamen.

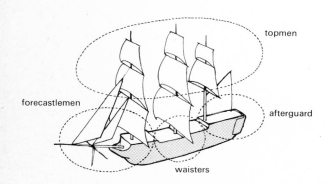

Working areas for the crew on watch.

Rating	Pay per lunar month
Handling of sails, sheets, braces and general duties	
Able seaman (AB)	£1 13s 6d
Ordinary seaman (OS)	£1 5s 6d
Landsman	£1 2s 6d

The highest rating reached by the majority of seamen was that of able seaman which was a reasonably secure position. The dirtiest and hardest tasks were performed by landsmen and OSs. ABs with some ambition and proven aptitude could hope to become one of the specialist 'crews':

BOATSWAIN'S CREW. General duties concerned with seamanship

Boatswain	£4 16s 0d on first-rate
	£3 1s 0d on sixth-rate
Boatswain's mate	£2 5s 6d on first-rate
	£1 16s 6d on sixth-rate
Yeoman of the boatswain's stores	£1 13s 6d

GUNNER'S CREW. Responsibility, shared with armourer, for maintenance of all guns, training of gun crews, condition of shot and powder, repair of guns.

Gunner	£4 16s 0d on first-rate
	£3 1s 0d on sixth-rate
Gunner's mate	£2 5s 6d on first-rate
	£1 16s 6d on sixth-rate
Yeoman of the powder room	£2 5s 6d
Quarter gunner	£1 16s 6d on first-rate
	£1 15s 6d on sixth-rate
Gunner's steward	£1 15s 6d on first-rate
	£1 9s 6d on sixth-rate
Gunner's tailor	£1 5s 6d

The gunner's steward and the tailor were, except on the largest ships, only ordinary seamen with no chance of promotion within the gunner's crew but they escaped the menial tasks of the other seamen.

CARPENTER'S CREW. In charge of the condition of the whole ship, repairs to hull and masts

Carpenter	£5 16s 0d on first-rate
	£3 1s 0d on sixth-rate
Carpenter's mate	£2 10s 6d on first-rate
	£2 0s 6d on sixth-rate
Carpenter's seaman	£1 16s 6d on first-rate
	£1 15s 6d on sixth-rate
Cooper	£1 13s 6d
Caulker	£2 10s 6d on first-rate
	£2 0s 6d on sixth-rate
Caulker's mate	£2 6s 6d on first-rate
	Rates of pay on lower rated ships not known

ARMOURER'S CREW

Armourer	£2 15s 6d on first-rate
	£2 0s 6d on sixth-rate
Armourer's mate	£2 5s 6d on first-rate
	£1 16s 6d on sixth-rate

ROPEMAKER'S CREW

Ropemaker	£2 10s 6d on first-rate
	£2 0s 6d on sixth-rate
Sailmaker	£2 5s 6d on first-rate
	£2 0s 6d on sixth-rate
Sailmaker's mate	£1 18s 6d
Sailmaker's crew	£1 15s 6d

QUARTERMASTER'S CREW. Steering the ship

Quartermaster	£2 5s 6d on first-rate
	£1 16s 6d on sixth-rate
Quartermaster's mate	£2 0s 6d on first-rate
	£1 15s 6d on sixth-rate

COOKS

Cook	£1 15s 6d on first-rate
	£1 14s 6d on sixth-rate
Captain's cook	£1 13s 6d
Cook's mate	£1 13s 6d

Captain's clerk	£4 7s 0d on first-rate
	£2 18s 6d on sixth-rate
Master's mate	£3 16s 6d on first-rate
	£2 12s 6d on sixth-rate
Master-at-arms	£2 15s 6d on first-rate
	£2 0s 6d on sixth-rate
Yeoman of the sheets	£2 2s 6d on first-rate
	£1 16s 6d on sixth-rate
Coxswain	£2 2s 6d on first-rate
	£1 16s 6d on sixth-rate
Trumpeter	£2 0s 6d on first-rate
	£1 14s 6d on sixth-rate
Ordinary trumpeter	£1 13s 6d
Captains of the forecastle, foretop, maintop, and afterguard	
	£2 0s 6d on first-rate
	£1 15s 6d on sixth-rate
Barber	£1 5s 6d

In ships with crewmen numbering in the hundreds there were many other and varied tasks. The list below gives a general picture of the type of tasks at which a seaman could find himself working:

Captain's sweeper, milkman and attendant to captain's cow, poulterer (fed geese in boats or hens in chicken coop), admiral's servant, captain's servant, second captain's servant, wardroom servant, painter, tailor, ship's barber, captain of the heads (in charge of cleaning toilet area in bows), assistant mate to the captain of the heads, hairdresser, assistant to purser and stewards, fifer, sentinel at sick bay, loblolly boy (assistant to surgeon) lady of the gunroom (reliable old AB who guarded the entrance to the wardroom and kept it clean), holders (worked in hold at stowing cargo and stores), wardroom cook, butcher, mast man (one to each mast to keep ropes coiled neatly and brasswork polished), writer to 1st lieutenant, pumpers (worked the bilge pumps).

All these tasks were for normal sailing conditions. Different tasks were allotted for battle stations.

Rewards and punishments

The landsmen were quickly falling into the strict routine of naval work and were accepting with resignation their new way of life. They had settled into friendly mess-gangs and many had found a pride in their section of work and tended to scorn other departments. The new friendships they had made and the money they hoped to receive when it was all over were their only rewards.

There was, however, another incentive offered by Their Lordships in London. This was prize money.

PRIZE MONEY. The Admiralty 'bought' any ship captured and the money was distributed among all those responsible for its capture. Strict rules controlled the sharing of the money. It was usually divided into eighths: the captain received two eighths, and the crewmen one eighth between them. The rest was shared between the officers and warrant-officers. If the ship was part of a fleet then the flag-officer also received a share, which was reasonable since the admiral bore the ultimate responsibility for the actions of the ship. Many seamen dreamed of the luck of *Caroline*, a 32-gun frigate, which captured a Spanish treasure ship, *San Raphael*, in January 1807. The captain received £50,000, the lieutenants £5,000 and ordinary seamen £200 each – enough to buy a house and some land. The commander of the fleet to which *Caroline* belonged was thousands of miles away at the time but he was equally delighted to find himself richer by £25,000. This was a rare case; normally seamen could expect about three or four pounds, and a lieutenant a few hundred.

The thought of prize money was probably one of the most important reasons for the dash and eagerness that was characteristic of British ships in clashes with the enemy.

PUNISHMENTS. The landsmen were taught methodically and firmly how to operate the ship and were soon expected to carry out orders immediately, thoroughly and without question. Allowances were made for the dull witted but otherwise no slacking was tolerated.

STARTING. This would probably be the first encounter with the force of authority that a newcomer would meet. The 'starter' was a short length of thick rope with a tight knot near the end, forming a type of pliable club. It was carried by each of the boatswain's crew. When an officer noticed a man who needed

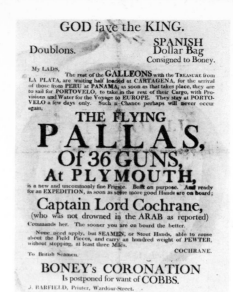

Posters like this seem to have had a strong appeal to sailors, who were mostly patriotic and anti-French. (Besides, since there was always the risk that they might be impressed and find themselves in a bad ship, it might be wise to volunteer to serve under a popular captain with a good chance of earning prize money.)

speeding up he would simply shout 'Start that man' and the nearest of the boatswain's crew would deliver a number of blows with the starter about the shoulders of the unlucky seaman. One or two blows were enough to make any man move fast and the punishment ceased at once. The starter was not used for prolonged beatings and it was not an official form of punishment authorised by the Admiralty.

GAGGING. The first reaction of men to hard authority was often an objection, but this was insubordination. Any lieutenant who considered a man to have been insubordinate or rude either in his speech or his manner could order him to be 'gagged'. The offender was tied loosely to the railings or shrouds and an iron marline-spike was put between his teeth and held there by a lashing around his head. He was left in this position until the officer ordered his release.

FLOGGING. Starting and gagging were enough to control most of the crew but men who were persistently lazy, drunk, careless or insubordinate were flogged. At 10.30 a.m. the master-at-arms paraded the offenders before the assembled crew while the marines lined the poop, the officers stood on the quarter deck and the surgeon prepared his medications. At 11.00 a.m. the captain came on deck with the list of offenders and gave the

This famous contemporary drawing, published in 1825, shows a typical assembly for flogging. The view is similar to the photograph on page 13 except that carronades are shown, not carriage guns. The central figure with his shirt removed appears to be confessing a crime to save an innocent man, (the title of the picture is 'The Point of Honour'). Note the seamen's dress and that of the two midshipmen.

order 'Rig the gratings' and a grating from a hatchway was set up against the ship's side. Each offender was told his crime and asked if he could offer any reasonable excuse. If the captain decided that punishment should be given he stated the number of lashes. The man was tied by his upraised arms to the grating and one of the boatswain's crew used a cat-o'-nine-tails to carry out the sentence. Three dozen lashes were accepted as normal for minor offences and more serious crimes carried three hundred. After the last cut the surgeon examined the man and gave medical treatment.

Written comments from the seamen of the day show that there was resentment amongst the crew if the number of lashes was excessive but they were also contemptuous and distrustful if the captain was lenient. Captains whose crews were happy and loyal were men who knew just how much punishment should be dealt out for each crime.

EAGLE. This was not used in all the fleets. It seems to have been a form of punishment given when flogging would have been too severe for the crime. The man was tied to the shrouds with arms and legs outspread and left to suffer the effects of rain, spray and wind for a number of hours.

FLOGGING ROUND THE FLEET. For more serious crimes, such as attempting to desert or striking an officer, the prisoner could be sentenced to a form of flogging that was almost a death sentence. When the fleet to which the vessel belonged came to anchor in port the offender was placed in a ship's boat and lashed to a capstan bar, then, with all crews brought on deck to watch, and with drums beating, he was rowed from ship to ship. At each ship he was given the ordered number of lashes. Those who survived such an ordeal were said to be physical and mental wrecks thereafter, but more often the man was dead before he reached the last ship.

RUNNING THE GAUNTLET. This punishment was reserved for seamen who stole from their shipmates and was administered by the crew themselves. The master-at-arms, with a marine to help him, guided the thief at bayonet point between the lines of seamen who lashed out at him with knotted rope yarns. Once a thief had run the gauntlet the affair was never referred to again.

Rewards were few and punishments were many, but after a few weeks the captain no longer had a mixed batch of landsmen, newcomers and old hands. Instead he had a crew. His crew now acted swiftly and surely, and his ship sailed steadily and finely wherever he ordered.

5 THE SHIP IN ACTION

Attacking the enemy

While the crew were learning how to manage the sailing machinery of their ship, they also went through rigorous practice, day after day, on how to handle the great guns. The captain could soon judge when the crew was proficient at ship handling but he knew there was no way to test their fighting abilities until the moment of their first battle. In a ship sailing alone – often a frigate – it was the captain's task to bring about that first battle and to do it in such a way that he could secure, and hold, all possible advantages over his enemy.

Positions of vantage

The captain of a frigate knew that his ship stood a very good chance of meeting an enemy vessel. Any such encounter would result in a 'single-ship' action, but he would be able to use the experience he gained, if he ever commanded a ship-of-the-line, in a fleet action. He knew the theory by heart. The French, with larger crews than the British, tended to try to dismast their foes to reduce their manoeuvrability, then to close in to fire carronades and small arms before boarding. The French courage and determination when boarding enemy ships had become legendary. The British captain, on the other hand, should be able to control his ship more smoothly and surely and use his guns at all ranges to pound the enemy into submission, only boarding if the foe did not submit.

When the lookout sighted a possible enemy sail on the horizon the captain mentally ran through the possible ways he could manoeuvre to gain favourable positions for inflicting maximum damage on the enemy ship.

CROSSING BOW OR STERN. If by careful sailing and counter-acting the enemy's movements he could cross the enemy's bows or stern the battle could be over in a few minutes. By keeping to

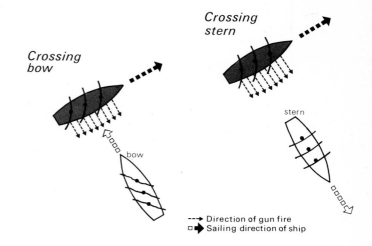

Crossing bow

Crossing stern

stern

bow

- - -▶ Direction of gun fire
□▪▶ Sailing direction of ship

windward he could control his ship, possibly reduce the wind on the enemy sails and each of his guns could fire as they bore on target. He could fire off about twenty shots with little chance of more than one or two shots in return. If his shots could strike the enemy's stern then they would smash through and wreak havoc as they travelled the length of the gun deck. A full broadside through a shattered stern would almost surely weaken the enemy beyond hope of recovery.

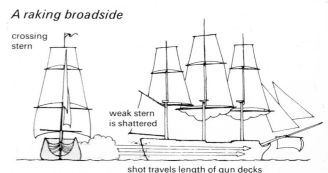

A raking broadside

crossing stern

weak stern is shattered

shot travels length of gun decks

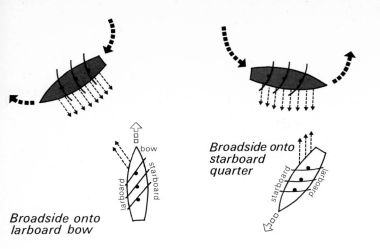

Broadside onto larboard bow

Broadside onto starboard quarter

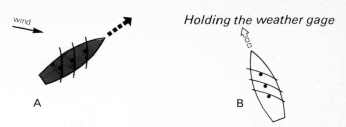

Holding the weather gage

A   B

Ship A holds the weather gage because it is running before the wind and is therefore fast and manoeuvrable. Ship B has the wind on the bows and has to tack to make progress. This makes it slower and less manoeuvrable unless it turns and flees.

BROADSIDE ONTO QUARTER OR BOW. If the captain misjudged and had to approach at an angle to the bow or stern he could still fire broadsides while the enemy could only bring a few guns to bear. This was more tricky since he would have to swing away fast or else a quick turn by an experienced foe would turn the attacker into the attacked. But it was probably worth the risk in order to be the first to pour on a broadside since the smoke, damage and confusion often prevented quick retaliation.

HOLDING THE WEATHER GAGE. Whatever the outcome of a battle the captain knew that his superiors would ask 'Did you hold the weather gage?' He knew that his answer must be 'Yes'. He would issue sailing orders immediately to ensure that as he closed in he would be upwind from his foe. This was the best attacking position. With the wind behind him he could move in speedily and wherever he chose. Holding the weather gage meant he could choose the time and method of his attack.

However, in bad weather being to windward had the disadvantage of putting the lower gun ports awash while the enemy's ports were clear. Even under good weather conditions the British guns would be depressed, but since they usually intended to smash the hull of the enemy this was not important. French naval tacticians did not always share the British desire to hold the weather position. Their liking for dismasting shots was suited to being in the leeward position since their guns would thus be elevated.

Firing on the run

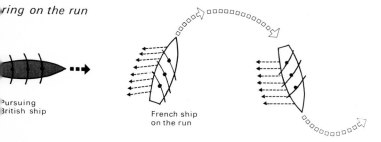

Pursuing British ship

French ship on the run

FIRING ON THE RUN. If the enemy captain had an experienced crew he might try making a run for it, knowing he was capable of firing on the run. The Frenchman could make a sudden half turn, fire a broadside, and be back on course before the British ship knew what had happened. This action could be repeated many times and the British ship could end up dismasted. But it could be counteracted by watching carefully and turning at the same time as the enemy ship to return the broadside.

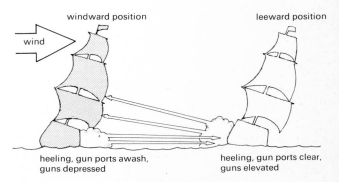

windward position   leeward position

wind

heeling, gun ports awash, guns depressed

heeling, gun ports clear, guns elevated

Clearing for action

The white speck on the horizon gradually grew in size until a midshipman with his telescope could make out the sail pattern, the hull shape and finally the tiny specks of blue, white and red of the Tricolour. She was a French frigate, her guns run out and ready for action. The days of training were over. The Admiralty could do no more to prepare them. All its trust now had to lie with the captain and his crew. The captain gave the order 'Beat to quarters'.

The rapid beating of the drum brought all work to a halt. The drum roll only lasted a few seconds and as it ceased the whole ship burst into a hurried, but carefully planned, activity. All the hammocks were neatly lashed and stowed in the hammock nettings around the ship's side; some were lashed to the lower section of the shrouds while others were lashed to form a protective barrier around each top. They formed effective walls to protect the crew from flying splinters, grape and musket shot. Huge nets were slung about five or six metres above the main deck to catch falling men, spars, or yards before they caused injury on the crowded deck. Other nets were hung along the side of the ship at deck level to hamper any attempt by the enemy to board.

Buckets of water were hauled aloft and the sails drenched with water. More buckets of water were placed at hatchways and beside each gun, and the decks were sprinkled with wet sand. The massive mainsail and any other sails not in use were furled and securely lashed. (This was known as reducing to battle canvas.) The yards were doubly secured by heavy chains to their masts.

Anything that might be a hindrance in battle had to be removed quickly to below the waterline, or else dropped overboard, and this included most of the animals. The butcher slaughtered any cows on board and their bodies were dropped over the side. Any goat pens or chicken coops went the same way, along with their occupants. It was usual to leave the hens in the ship's boats and the pigs in the 'manger' (see page 13).

Below decks the carpenter and his crew were steadily and ruthlessly clearing away the wooden partitions of the officers' quarters and hurrying them into the hold while others passed down the captain's furniture. Any item that could not be quickly stowed below was thrown over the side. Seamen cleared all their personal belongings from the mess decks. Nothing, no matter how valuable, was allowed to interfere with the fighting efficiency of the ship.

Soon the gun crews were by their guns and checking the equipment. A large body of marines positioned themselves on the poop deck while others took up stations on the forecastle or guarded the hatchways to the lower deck. The surgeon's assistants placed a pile of tourniquets beside each gun while, below, the cockpit was turned into a hospital and operating theatre. Trunks and cases belonging to the junior officers were carefully arranged with tarpaulins thrown over them to form resting and waiting couches for the wounded. The large dining table was cleared and scrubbed down and lanterns hung above. This was now the operating table where the only anaesthetic was a glass of rum and a piece of leather to bite upon. As the experienced seamen hurried about their tasks they made their friends promise to throw them overboard if they were seriously wounded. Better to die quickly than suffer on the 'table'.

The carpenter and his crew brought prepared waddings and shot plugs to be used for plugging shot holes in the hull near or below the waterline. Their function during battle was to patrol the decks and repair any damage that could impair the operation of the ship. The gunner opened the magazine (the ammunition store) and ensured that the candles in the adjoining candle room were lit. He checked that those working in the magazine wore felt slippers and carried no metal objects. The blankets covering the entrance were wetted and a marine took up his post as guard. Cartridges of powder were issued to the powder monkeys queueing at the entrance and fresh cartridges were filled with powder.

The galley fire was extinguished, small arms, pikes and axes were made ready for the boarding parties, a ship's boat, usually slung over the stern, was lowered and towed astern, officers checked each deck and reported when all was ready. On the quarter deck behind the mainmast the signal officers and clerical assistants gathered near the captain.

The time from the first roll of the drum till the moment when all was ready for battle was only a few minutes. Now, in absolute silence, the ship drew nearer the enemy.

Serving the guns

Below on the main gun deck the bulk of the crew and their officers stood ready by their guns. The ports were open, the

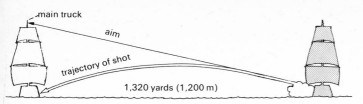

Main truck aiming

When intending to hit a ship-of-the-line at about 1,320 yards (1,200 m) distance on the waterline the gunner aimed at the enemy's main truck.

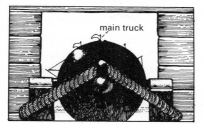

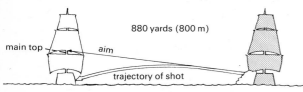

Main top aiming

When intending to hit a ship-of-the-line at 880 yards (800 m) distance on the waterline the gunner aimed at the enemy's main top.

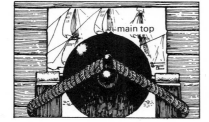

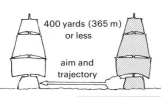

Open sights

Anything nearer than 400 yards (365 m) was usually considered as point blank range and aim was direct. Broadsides were given at less than 300 yards (275 m) when possible.

guns loaded and run out on both sides. If the ship altered course the gun crew would have to man the gun on the other side of the ship.

Through the open ports some could glimpse the approaching enemy and try to judge the moves and countermoves of their captain as both ships tacked and tacked again in bluff and counterbluff. But all the time the gap was narrowing. At a mile (1.6 km) distance, the order came for the first ranging shot. The master gunner chose his gun, took careful aim, and the ball of iron sped out, bouncing over the waves to pass under the enemy bows. An answering billow of smoke signalled the return fire which passed overhead with a soft whistle. As the range narrowed down from 1,320 yards to 880 yards (1,200 m to 800 m) the guns went into action and there was no more time to watch. Guns were sponged, loaded, aimed and fired amidst a deafening roar. Smoke filled the gun deck as the massive guns recoiled and rumbled backwards until held by their breech ropes. For those engaged in their first battle it was a mad terrifying world only half seen through stinging eyes and half heard through ringing ears. Warrant-officers pushed dazed men into their positions or flung them aside from the crushing wheels of the gun carriages. Half-blinded and deaf men, working mechanically at the gun tackles, found their feet

The gunner directs his crew to use handspikes to slew (swing) the loaded gun to the left. To show the positions clearly the artist has spaced the men well apart. The picture on the front cover is closer to the crowded reality.

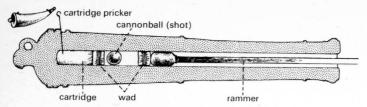

After the barrel had been swabbed to remove any burning fragments from the previous cartridge, the new cartridge was rammed home, followed by a wad and shot; a second wad held the shot in position. The cartridge pricker was pushed down the touch hole to pierce the canvas of the cartridge and fine priming powder was poured from the powder horn into the hole. A lighted 'match' (twisted cotton wicks which burned slowly) was applied to the touch hole to fire the gun.

slipping on blood-stained decks. Enemy shots were striking home and hurling both guns and men across the decks in a tangle of wreckage. Razor-sharp daggers of splintered wood hummed through the black smoke and men fell screaming.

The friendly mess deck of yesterday had become a scene from the worst of their nightmares, but there was nowhere to hide. Officers stood over them with drawn sword and pistol while grim-faced marines, with fingers on the trigger, allowed only the young powder monkeys access to the gangways. Kicked and buffeted into action by the senior ratings, the gun crews dragged bodies clear of wreckage and heaved them through the gun ports. As their friends vanished through the ports some noticed that the horizon had gone. Instead there was a wall of wood broken at intervals by black squares holding menacing gun muzzles. The enemy ship was now only yards away.

Boarding

The British captain's tactics had worked well. In the running gun battle he had suffered damage to masts and sails and taken a few heavy blows to the hull but he had pounded away at the hull of the Frenchman. The enemy's deck was heaped with wreckage and her sides had gaping holes. Blood was running from the scupper holes and her firing rate had fallen drastically. She was in a bad way. It was time to board.

A few rounds of chain shot fired from close range shredded her sails and cut most of her shrouds. She was helpless now and could not escape. A turn of the wheel brought the ship swinging in towards her foe while the carronades of the forecastle destroyed whole sections of the enemy deck. Seconds later the two ships ground together, their upper rigging, completely entangled, locking them side by side. Separated now by only a few feet the main guns fired on, the wood on both ships charring and even bursting into flames in some parts. Men previously detailed as boarders had been called to collect weapons and now, on the command 'Boarders away' they surged over the protective hammocks and fought to cross to the enemy and gain a foothold. Ranks of marines fired volleys, and marksmen fired from the tops or lit grenades and heaved them down towards the foe. Men climbed through the lower ports and attempted to enter the French gun deck; others, more agile, ran along the main spars into the enemy rigging.

Men fought each other with muskets, bayonets, pistols, knives, cutlasses, pikes, axes, and fists. Although they had suffered terrible casualties from the British gun fire, the French fought ferociously. The fight was bitter, desperate and savage but it could not last long. With most of their officers dead, the French colours were hauled down and the wounded captain handed his sword to his conqueror.

Aftermath

Once the enemy crew had been disarmed and placed under guard the ships had to be cleaned up. Round shot had chopped down masts and smashed sections of the ship's sides into jagged splinters. Rigging and spars hung like broken branches. On the orlop deck the surgeon did what he could for the wounded. His domain was the only place where rank and its privileges were ignored. Here 'first come' was 'first served', officers waited their turn behind cabin boys for the attention of the surgeon's knife.

The dead from the boarding struggle were dropped over the side while those who remained unscathed set about repairing the damage and sorting out the confusion of ropes, wood and shredded hammocks. The pumps were operated and the blood washed away but its smell could only be cleared by swabbing the decks with vinegar and brimstone. The galley fires were relit, meals taken and finally there was some rest and sleep. Perhaps the first lieutenant remained awake and active, trying to

Nelson boarding San Nicolas *on 14 February 1797 during the battle of Cape St Vincent. Despite the theatrical poses imagined by the artist the general picture is a good presentation of the conditions of boarding.*

impress his captain, and hoping to be made prize captain. Many of the crew made calculations of how much prize money was due to them, but others sat dazed, deaf and bewildered, still shaking from their ordeal. Their first sea battle was over, and they were still alive.

Jobs for frigates

The fast and powerful frigates captured the imagination of seamen and public alike. Not bound by the strict discipline of fleet formations, the captain could act with enterprise and decisiveness. Frigates performed many tasks during the war.

CONVOY WORK. They shepherded the vital convoys of merchantmen from around the world and fought many single-ship actions against pirates, privateers and enemy men-of-war. They could outsail any ship-of-the-line (very necessary since one of them could blow a frigate out of the water) but they were capable of standing and fighting any other type of ship.

SCOUTING. Whenever a fleet patrolled or sailed into new water the frigates became the eyes and ears of the admiral. Scouting many miles ahead, like light cavalry on land, they quickly reported all they saw. They captured small traders and fishermen and interrogated the crews; they crept close inshore and observed defences and activity in enemy harbours; they examined shore lines and plotted landing spots. They were the 'intelligence officers' of the fleets; an admiral without his frigates was blind.

RAIDING. Frigates were ideal for small punitive expeditions against the occupied mainland. Remote French signal stations often fell prey to the speedy frigates. Most of these stations were guarded by gun batteries and a camp of infantry was usually close by. In darkness, and a mile or two (a few kilometres) down the coast from the station, the ship's boats landed marines, sailors, and some 8-pound (3.6 kg) cannon. The ship would make a sudden attack on the station, pounding away with broadsides, while the landing party made a surprise attack in the rear. If successful, a forced entry would enable explosives, with a time fuse, to be planted in the signal tower. If all went well, the landing party would return with prisoners, the tower would be destroyed, and the ship sailing away before French troops could arrive on the scene.

CUTTING OUT. Many a free-roving frigate off the French coast could see the masts of the enemy, safe within bays and harbours. If the enemy refused to come out then the only way to capture them was to go in and get them. This operation was called 'cutting out' and involved a well-trained boarding party rowing into the harbour undetected, taking the ship by surprise, and then sailing it out to sea.

A very successful cutting out was made by *Pallas* (page 26) on 5 April 1806. She had spotted two 14-gun brigantines anchored close to guard forts in the Gironde estuary that led to Bordeaux.

Pallas pulled well away from the coast and when darkness fell the boarding parties rowed 20 miles (24 km) back to land and into the estuary. An hour or two before sunrise the attack was made. One of the brigantines was captured and her sails set. As dawn broke she was speeding out to sea pursued by the second brigantine and under fire from the shore batteries. Two hours later the cutting-out team had rejoined *Pallas* with their prize. The only casualties had been three men wounded.

Some unexpected factors

The sailing qualities of the British seaman and the expert use of the great guns brought success after success in single-ship actions and confidence in British sea-power grew strong. The French were no easy prey and there were losses, but the general pattern was one of British superiority. This great confidence was sometimes shattered by unexpected factors. Nothing in war can be taken for granted; things can go suddenly wrong.

Only a month after her cutting out in the Gironde estuary *Pallas* sailed into Aix Roads to tempt out the French ships sheltering there. The challenge was taken up by the French *Minerva*, with twice the fire-power of *Pallas*, and three brigantines. *Pallas* engaged *Minerva* so close that the shore batteries dared not fire and the brigantines were held off by skilled manoeuvring. After two hours' battle *Minerva*'s guns fell silent and *Pallas* closed in to board. Victory seemed certain.

The French conquest of Europe had ensured a good supply of oak for her ships and *Minerva* was solidly built. Britain, with her supply of European oak cut off, had many ships built of light fir. *Pallas* was one of them. As she swung in she struck *Minerva* heavily and the light wood of the British ship stove in. With sprung masts (cracked and loosened in their sockets) and leaking heavily, *Pallas* abandoned her prize and headed for open waters, her pumps working continuously to keep her afloat.

A more shattering blow came when British frigates fought American frigates in the short war of 1812. With Britain holding 124 frigates and the Americans only 8 the naval strength of the United States seemed negligible. But the Americans had built very large, fast and powerful frigates that carried fifty-six guns with a broadside weight of 768 pounds (350 kg). Solidly built with the captain present during construction, and manned by carefully selected volunteers (some being

Two British 36-gun frigates, San Fiorenzo *and* La Nymphe *(both originally French ships, captured in the early years of the war), tackle two French ships,* Résistance *and* Constance, *off Brest on 9 March 1797. The* Résistance *of 40 guns (centre fore) struck her colours after twenty minutes and the* Constance *of 22 guns (right distance) struck ten minutes later. The fact that all ships are carrying a full spread of sails shows that this was a fast moving action. The picture was painted by Nicholas Pocock.*

British deserters who would be hanged if captured), they proved to be formidable foes. Moreover, the Americans had copied the British gun drill and were very well disciplined, whereas by 1812 some British crews were becoming less brisk and conscientious in carrying out their orders.

There were some British victories, and eventually the American ships were taken or blockaded, but the cost in casualties was very high and the larger American frigates, such as *Constitution* which destroyed *Guerriere* in August of 1812 and captured *Java* in December, proved to be far too powerful for British frigates. The Admiralty issued firm orders that no British frigate was to engage one of the larger American frigates in a single-ship action.

6 THE WORK OF THE FLEETS

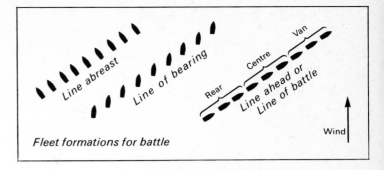

Fleet formations for battle

Fleet procedures

Promotion, retirement, or death from sickness or enemy action among the captains of the ships-of-the-line meant that our frigate captain would probably have to say farewell in the end to the active and stimulating life of the frigates to take his place as captain of a 74 in one of the main fleets. With his independent judgement restricted he would have to adjust to the close command of an admiral and the strict, slow and ponderous movements of the battle lines. His consolation was facing the reality that frigate actions were only skirmishes compared to the meeting of opposing fleets. Fleet actions were directly linked to the general overall strategy of economic and land warfare, and a destroyed fleet could mean a defeated nation. The fates of armies and nations many miles away hung in the balance when the giant ships-of-the-line edged their way into battle.

Under the command of its admiral the fleet moved as a single unit with written, predetermined, plans of attack and defence. Standing orders were issued to each ship and were only overridden by signals from the flagship. Keeping formation was vital and the progression of the whole fleet had to be geared down to the individual sailing characteristics of the slowest ship. This tended to make the movements of fleets appear slow and cumbersome.

Captains read their instructions from the admiral and checked them against written Fighting Instructions with which they had been issued, perhaps comparing their orders with sections such as Paragraph VII:

'When the signal to form a line of bearing for either tack is made, the ships (whatever course they may be directed to steer) are to place themselves in such a manner that if they were to haul to the wind together on the tack for which the line of bearing is formed, they would immediately form a line of battle on that tack. To do this, every ship must bring the ship which would be her second ahead, if the line of

battle were formed, to bear on that point of the compass on which the line of battle would sail, viz., on that point of the compass which is seven points from the direction of the wind, or six points if the signal is made to keep *close* to the wind.

'As the intention of a line of bearing is to keep the fleet ready to form suddenly a line of battle, the position of the division or squadron flags, shown with the signal for such a line, will refer to the forming of the line of battle; that division or squadron whose flag is uppermost (without considering whether it do or do not form the van of the line of bearing) is to place itself in that station which would become the van if the fleet should haul to the wind and form the line of battle; and the division whose flag is undermost is to place itself in that station in which it would become the rear if by hauling to the wind the line of battle should be formed.'

Our captain sweated over the correct interpretation of his written orders, and feared his admiral's displeasure more than the guns of the enemy.

The fleets in action

The map on page 9 shows the general positions of the blockading fleets. For the men involved, the months of blockade dragged on into years. Through all the seasons the fleets sailed up and down their allotted stations while their frigates scuttled back and forth with information and orders. Attempts were constantly made to bring the enemy into action but engagements were rare. There could be no relaxing, for the aim was not to bottle up the enemy fleets but to engage them with superior odds and destroy them. So the blockade wearily continued, waiting for the day when the French and their allies finally made a decisive move and put to sea in force. Each day that dawned could be the day when the enemy made that move.

A SMALL FLEET ACTION WHILE ON BLOCKADE. In June 1795 Admiral Cornwallis was on blockade duty in the English Channel with a small section of the Channel Fleet, *Royal Sovereign*, 100 guns, *Bellerophon*, *Mars*, *Triumph* and *Brunswick*, each with 74 guns, and the frigates *Phaeton*, *Pallas* and *Kingfisher*. The main fleet lay somewhere to the west under the command of Lord Bridport. The French were expecting a convoy from the Indies, so a fleet of 30 ships, 13 ships-of-the-line, 14 frigates, 2 brigantines and a cutter slipped out from Brest under the command of Admiral Villaret-Joyeuse. They intended to meet the convoy and escort it home; instead they sighted Cornwallis's fleet. The British, being hopelessly outnumbered, turned and fled westwards, hoping to lead the French into the main British fleet. The French gave chase.

It was soon clear that *Bellerophon* and *Brunswick* were sluggish in the water and were falling behind, so Cornwallis ordered them to lighten ship. Over the side went all the anchors, the ships' boats and all the water stored on board. This helped a little but the French were still gaining on them. Cornwallis could not leave the two ships to certain destruction so *Royal Sovereign*, *Mars* and *Triumph* fell in behind their slower comrades while *Phaeton* sped ahead hoping to contact the main fleet. The small British group was now committed to the speed of *Bellerophon* and *Brunswick* and soon the leading French ships were firing their ranging shots.

The two slow 74s now started lightening in earnest. Bread, meat, sails, and spars were dumped and finally the carronades and spare shot went overboard. But it was not enough and soon the rearmost British were engaged in running fights with the leading French ships. After four hours of this *Mars* received damage that made her drop astern. Cornwallis turned the small fleet to rally around *Mars* and the French closed in to finish them off.

The frigate *Phaeton*, now miles ahead, played the last card in Cornwallis's hand. Knowing that the French knew the British codes, she sent a false signal saying she could see three ships ahead, then that she could see five, then nine, and finally she let fly her topsails to indicate a full fleet in sight. At the same time

the French on the wings of the battle area sighted dozens of sails on the horizon (it was in fact a British merchant convoy heading for home). Villaret assumed that he was heading straight into the British main Channel Fleet and promptly turned and headed for Brest.

Cornwallis had saved his ships by trickery and it was a moral defeat for the French. Yet, because of the action of Villaret in chasing Cornwallis, the route home for the French convoy was cleared and it reached its destination safely, so, in a practical way, it was a French success.

THE DESTRUCTION OF A FLEET. In 1798 the Mediterranean Fleet received news that the French were preparing an invasion force in Toulon (see page 9). This could have been the first stage in a French breakout and invasion of Britain and, under the command of Rear-Admiral Nelson, the fleet headed for Toulon. Storms delayed their passage and when they arrived off Toulon in May the port was deserted. A desperate search followed, hampered by a lack of frigates, but finally they tracked the French down to Egypt where Napoleon had landed his troops, and already conquered the country. The French fleet was anchored in Aboukir Bay, about fifteen miles (24 km) from Alexandria. With fourteen ships-of-the-line the British fleet hove to and examined the thirteen French ships-of-the-line anchored in an almost solid line inside the bay. They were lined up bow to stern with no room for enemy ships to break through. They formed a wall, bristling with guns. It was the afternoon of

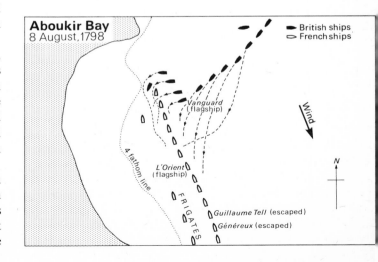

Aboukir Bay
8 August, 1798

■ British ships
□ French ships

Vanguard (flagship)

Wind

N

4 fathom line

L'Orient (flagship)

FRIGATES

Guillaume Tell (escaped)
Généreux (escaped)

The Battle of the Nile, pictured from directly astern of the anchored French line of battle as the first British ship rounds the far end. Nicholas Pocock painted the scene within a few months of the battle and, although he was not an eyewitness, he had expert knowledge of ships and gives a vivid impression of the scene at the moment that decided the battle.

8 August and if the British were to do anything they would have to do it quickly, before the French could make their already strong position even stronger. At four in the afternoon the British attacked.

With dusk approaching, the French did not expect an attack until the next morning. Many of the guns which were being placed in batteries on the horns of the bay were not yet positioned and some of the ships' crews were working ashore. On the ships the guns which faced shoreward were still lashed and the gun ports were closed, because any attack was bound to come from the seaward side only. But their strong position had one small weakness. Between the French left flank and the shore there was a narrow but navigable gap. It was hard to detect, but the British spotted it and headed straight towards it. At the last moment they split into two sections; one turned and sailed along the outside of the French line while the other passed through the gap and went along the inside. Secured firmly in line and attacked from both sides the French stood little chance. The British ships could move steadily down both sides of the line at will, bringing overwhelming fire-power against each section in turn. The result was a complete victory for Nelson. He took ten prizes and only two French ships escaped, one of them carrying Admiral Villeneuve. The French

flagship, *L'Orient*, was set on fire and blew up in the most spectacular explosion ever seen in those days.

The campaign of Trafalgar

After almost twelve years of war, the first months of 1805 saw little change in the general situation. On the continent of Europe the brilliant and active Napoleon Bonaparte seemed invincible. At sea the British fleets controlled the trade routes and continued the wearisome blockade. When opposing ships met, the British were usually successful, but still the main French fleets remained intact, sheltering under the protection of harbour defences. The French sea-power was not destroyed, it lay dormant, ready at any time to combine into an overwhelming force that could smash its way into the Channel and clear the way for the invasion of England.

On 2 March 1805 Napoleon Bonaparte issued orders that were to bring the stalemate at sea to its dramatic climax. Napoleon was a great tactician and strategist with a superb sense of timing. However he was no seaman and never fully grasped the problems affecting timing at sea where, even regardless of British ships, the weather alone could make sudden reversals of plans necessary. Napoleon expected his orders to be obeyed without question. He expected his admirals to overcome all obstacles, no matter how impossible. Any admiral needs authority and confidence to adapt or alter general instructions according to the prevailing conditions, but Napoleon never allowed his admirals such freedom.

Admiral Pierre Villeneuve, now aged 41, was an experienced seaman and ardent revolutionary. He commanded the main French fleet in Toulon. He knew that his ships and men looked good in port but he also knew that the men had had little experience of handling their ships and fighting. Unlike the British they had not been trained by years of blockading in all weathers. Villeneuve's previous objections to the Emperor's orders had earned him the Emperor's anger, and when new orders arrived in March 1805 he dared not refuse to obey. Reluctantly he prepared his fleet for sea.

Napoleon's orders

To Napoleon Bonaparte the orders that he issued on 20 March 1805 to his fleets were logical and strategically sound. A massive army with its hundreds of troop transports was ready and waiting on the northern coast of France. The French fleets were now to break out, escape the blockading British without fighting, and then to combine forces. They would then ensure a safe passage for the invasion flotilla. The details were, in a simplified form, as follows:

Admiral Ganteaume in Brest with twenty-one ships-of-the-line and six frigates was to break out and head for Ferrol. There he was to drive off the small British squadron and allow the French and Spanish ships at Ferrol to clear port and join forces with him. This combined fleet was to elude any large British force and head across the Atlantic to the West Indies and cruise off Martinique.

Admiral Villeneuve in Toulon with eleven ships-of-the-line and six frigates was to leave the port undetected, avoid the Mediterranean Fleet of Nelson, sail to Cadiz, drive off the small blockading fleet, liberate the Spanish ships, and then head for Martinique.

Admiral Missiessy, who had already slipped out of Rochefort, was to avoid contact with the British and sail for Martinique.

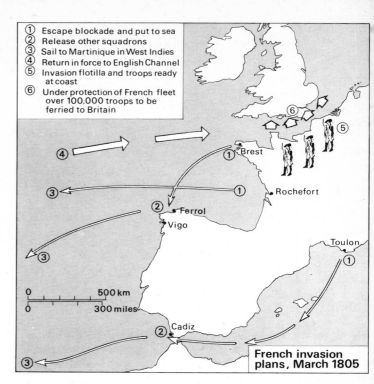

① Escape blockade and put to sea
② Release other squadrons
③ Sail to Martinique in West Indies
④ Return in force to English Channel
⑤ Invasion flotilla and troops ready at coast
⑥ Under protection of French fleet over 100,000 troops to be ferried to Britain

French invasion plans, March 1805

Strategically the French invasion plan was good but there were a number of weak points at the tactical level, especially in the timing of the escaping fleets and the meeting in the West Indies. The problem of escape was not so difficult, since the British were tending more and more to employ the 'open blockade' which meant they were deliberately keeping well out of sight to try to tempt the French to put to sea. Once they reached open water the British were ready to pounce in force.

Any other French or Spanish ships in Europe and the West Indies had to rendezvous at Martinique.

Once assembled in the West Indies the fleet, expected to number about eighty ships-of-the-line and more than twelve frigates, was to recross the Atlantic to Ushant and thence sweep up the English Channel. Such a fleet could smash any British resistance.

To conserve forces for the final battle in the English Channel all admirals were instructed to avoid clashing with any large British force.

CARRYING OUT NAPOLEON'S ORDERS. Napoleon's instructions to escape but not to fight caused trouble almost at once. Admiral Ganteaume in Brest with twenty-one ships-of-the-line found about fifteen British ships outside Brest. He wanted to fight his way out but the numbers meant a major battle, so he checked with Napoleon. The answer was, as in the orders, escape but escape unseen without a battle. Ganteaume made attempts to escape, but each time the British fleet appeared quickly on the scene and he returned to port. He never got out and the fleet remained in Brest. The admiral's sailing in and out of Brest made him the laughing stock of those unaware of his strict orders. The ships in Ferrol waited in vain for his arrival.

Admiral Missiessy, who was already at sea, had no trouble in reaching the West Indies where he awaited the arrival of Admiral Villeneuve. By May no one had arrived so he sailed back to Rochefort.

On 30 March Villeneuve left Toulon. Sailing east and then south between the Balearic Islands, Villeneuve succeeded in dodging Nelson and, in the second week of April, reached Cadiz where the Spanish Admiral, Gravina, brought his fleet out. Together they headed for Martinique. Admiral Villeneuve had successfully carried out the first part of his orders.

Villeneuve reached the West Indies but could find no sign of other French fleets (Missiessy had nearly reached Rochefort by now). It was now that he received fresh orders from Napoleon.

ORDERS FROM NAPOLEON TO VILLENEUVE, MAY 1805.

Spend a month damaging or capturing British possessions in the West Indies.

Sail to Ferrol, release the blockaded ships and then carry on to Brest to free Ganteaume.

The combined fleets will enter the Channel as previously planned.

The British needed no new orders to cope with the situation. All had been planned beforehand by the Admiralty. The main Channel Fleet was on station bottling up the French in Brest. Villeneuve had escaped and had not been destroyed, this was disturbing news but the Admiralty could rely on their admirals to act according to the general plan. They knew that Nelson would pursue Villeneuve and attempt to destroy him. Failing that, they knew that he would be sure to return to the Channel, ready to take part in the last stand against invasion.

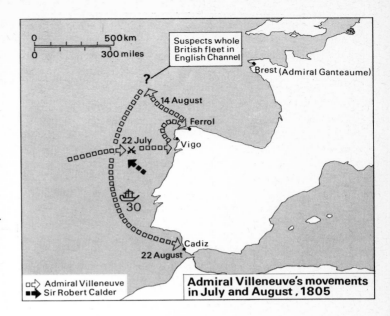

Admiral Villeneuve's movements in July and August, 1805

Admiral Villeneuve
Sir Robert Calder

Without issuing any further orders Their Lordships could rely on every available British ship to arrive in the Channel in time to face any large-scale French threat. Unlike the French every British captain understood the overall plan and could be relied upon to act accordingly.

Reluctantly Villeneuve obeyed his new orders. He was ignorant of the British fleet movements; the French and Spanish fleets did not work as a team – his relationship with the Spanish admiral was not good; and he would have preferred Ganteaume to be free of Brest before he entered the waters of northern Biscay. In early June he learned that Nelson had followed him across the Atlantic and was already in the West Indies searching for him. He abandoned his work in the islands and headed east towards Ferrol. The voyage turned out to be difficult, with adverse weather conditions, and took nearly a month during which time about a thousand men died. When nearing Ferrol his damaged ships and sick men met a British squadron under Sir Robert Calder on the 22 July. The battle, fought in fog, was inconclusive and Villeneuve withdrew to Vigo with only slight losses. By 14 August Villeneuve had repaired his damage and freed the ships in Ferrol. Now, with a fleet of thirty ships-of-the-line, he was lying off the north coast of Spain, and wondering what to do.

To press on northwards now seemed impossible. Ganteaume was still locked up in Brest and by now the whole British fleet would know what was happening and would probably be waiting in full force at the mouth of the Channel. To move north would mean the destruction of his fleet. So Villeneuve turned south and on 22 August entered Cadiz. On 27 August Napoleon Bonaparte ordered his army of invasion to break camp and march to Austria. The threat to Britain of imminent invasion was over.

In Cadiz, on 28 September, Villeneuve received instructions to enter the Mediterranean, disembark troops at Naples, and then return to Toulon. He set about preparing the combined French and Spanish fleets for the operation.

The final moves

The French fleets were once more pinned down. The fleet in Brest could make no move until released by the Cadiz force so attention now focused on Admiral Villeneuve. A British fleet of twenty-seven ships-of-the-line converged on Cadiz where the combined Spanish and French fleets numbered thirty-three ships-of-the-line. Action was expected since this was probably the last chance for the French to move, either into the Mediterranean or to the coast of England or Ireland, before an overwhelming force of British ships blockaded them once more.

Early on the morning of 19 October, Villeneuve made his move. Light winds caused considerable delays and it was not until the 20th that the last ships cleared the harbour. By 4 p.m. on the 20th the fleet was sailing south-east towards the Straits of Gibraltar. Nelson's fleet lay to the south-west, sixty miles (96 km) from Cadiz. Frigates and sloops watched every move of the French and reported swiftly to the main fleet. By first light on 21 October the fleets were in sight of each other. The French were in line heading south-east off Cape Trafalgar when, closing in from the west with the wind astern, came the British fleet in two lines.

Villeneuve's fleet had straggled into a disorderly line and he realised that if he continued his van would probably escape untouched into the Mediterranean but his centre and rear would be lost. The only way to meet the British as a full battle fleet was to reverse course. At 8.30 a.m. he gave the order to turn and head north-west.

The British fleet bore slowly down at about two knots in two

11.50 a.m., 21 Oct. 1805. The first shots:
Fougueux (French) opens fire on
Royal Sovereign (British)

parallel lines led by Nelson in *Victory* in the northern line and by Collingwood in *Royal Sovereign* in the southern line. The French prepared for battle with eager patriotism. The Spanish, distrustful of their French allies, were uncertain. The British expected losses but were confident of victory. Ten minutes before noon, at a range of 1,000 yards (900 m), *Fougueux* (French) fired the first shots of the battle – a broadside at the oncoming *Royal Sovereign* and the first British casualties fell.

The battle

Thousands of words would be needed to describe the Battle of Trafalgar. All that can be done in these pages is to outline the pattern of events.

Nelson's plan was to use the two heavy first-rates, *Victory* and *Royal Sovereign*, as battering rams to break through the French centre. These two ships would have to bear the full broadsides from five or six ships-of-the-line without being able

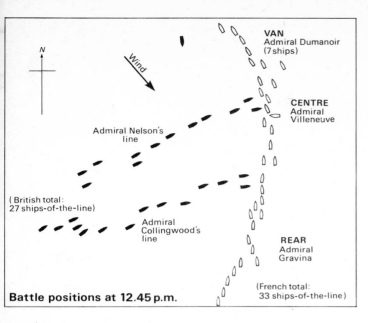

Wind

VAN
Admiral Dumanoir
(7 ships)

CENTRE
Admiral
Villeneuve

Admiral Nelson's
line

(British total:
27 ships-of-the-line)

Admiral Collingwood's
line

REAR
Admiral
Gravina

(French total:
33 ships-of-the-line)

Battle positions at 12.45 p.m.

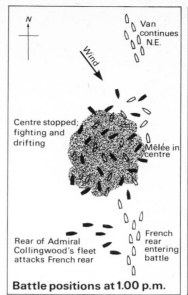

Wind

Van
continues
N.E.

Centre stopped;
fighting and
drifting

Mêlée in
centre

Rear of Admiral
Collingwood's fleet
attacks French rear

French
rear
entering
battle

Battle positions at 1.00 p.m.

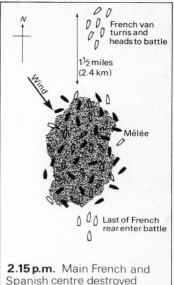

Wind

French van
turns and
heads to battle

1½ miles
(2.4 km)

Mêlée

Last of French
rear enter battle

2.15 p.m. Main French and
Spanish centre destroyed

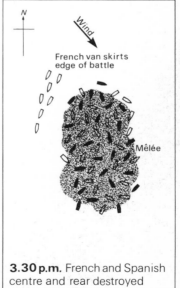

Wind

French van skirts
edge of battle

Mêlée

3.30 p.m. French and Spanish
centre and rear destroyed

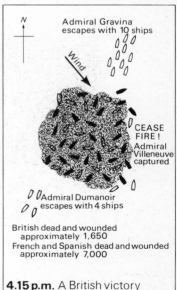

Admiral Gravina
escapes with 10 ships

Wind

CEASE
FIRE!
Admiral
Villeneuve
captured

Admiral Dumanoir
escapes with 4 ships

British dead and wounded
approximately 1,650
French and Spanish dead and wounded
approximately 7,000

4.15 p.m. A British victory

to return fire until actually passing through the line. It was a calculated risk and assumed that the Franco-Spanish fire would be slow and not very accurate. The plan worked, but both ships suffered heavy damage on the final half-mile (800 m) run. *Victory* had twenty men killed and thirty wounded before she fired a shot. Both ships were able to repay the damage with their first shots into the sterns of their foes as they passed through the line. *Victory*'s first broadside, including carronades, into the stern of Villeneuve's flagship, *Bucentaure*, caused 200 casualties and dismounted twenty guns.

The rest of the British lines of ships slowly followed their leaders into the Franco-Spanish centre and oncoming rear. The battle was now in full swing and it was up to individual captains to find a foe and fight. The intention was for the main force of British ships to destroy the Franco-Spanish centre before its rear could join in and before its van could turn and reverse course into the battle. If the Franco-Spanish van had made an immediate reversal then the British task would have been extremely difficult. As it was, Admiral Dumanoir with his van of seven ships continued to sail northwards, did not turn until 2.15 p.m., and at 3.30 had still not reached the main battle.

By 2.15 p.m. the Franco-Spanish centre was scattered and the British could face the rear ships as they sailed into the fray. At

3.30 p.m. it was clear that the centre and rear had been defeated and Dumanoir with his van had not yet entered the battle. At 4.15 p.m. the signal to cease fire was hoisted from *Victory* and at

4.30 the last guns were fired. Gravina with ten ships was fleeing to the north and Dumanoir with four ships was heading southwest. The British, with nineteen enemy ships-of-the-line captured or destroyed, had won the day.

THE MÊLÉE. Nelson's tactics ensured the best odds for his ships, but the final reckoning had to be in the free-for-all, the mêlée. This was where the individual captains sailed into the battle smoke to find a foe and to destroy him. Determined and confident they searched for targets.

The Spanish were not keen to fight for French interests and were distrustful of Villeneuve's management. But the eighteen French ships were surging with enthusiasm and determination. Despite the British advantage gained by their method of attack is was to be no easy victory. In the smoke-shrouded battle, ships weaved amongst friend and foe, and fired when they could. Ships collided or rammed each other. They lay alongside each other with spars and rigging entangled. Single ships found themselves fired upon by six or more of the enemy. Some searched for almost an hour before they had a clear line of fire and would not hit friend as well as foe. Once four ships-of-the-line, two French and two British, lay like a huge raft, their rigging enmeshed together. White gun smoke rolled around in thick clouds and many battling pairs of ships felt themselves to be alone and cut off from their comrades.

Elsewhere in this book we have described the normal battle procedures, but the battle off Cape Trafalgar produced some unusual situations. One example is the incident in which Nelson was fatally wounded. *Victory*, with its three decks of 104 guns rammed the French *Redoutable*, a two decker of 74 guns under the command of Captain Lucas, and the two ships swung alongside each other. *Redoutable*'s gun ports were slammed shut and Lucas ordered almost all his men on deck where they set up a deadly hail of musket fire and threw hundreds of grenades onto the open decks of *Victory*. Nelson fell wounded and in ten minutes most of *Victory*'s crew had retreated to the main gun decks below. It was a strange situation. Below, the main guns of *Victory* were smashing the empty hull of *Redoutable*, many shots passing straight through her. Above, the Frenchmen faced the almost deserted deck of *Victory* and prepared to board. Spar lashings were cut and the fallen timbers made a bridge across to *Victory*. *Victory* was now firing her guns downwards in an attempt to sink *Redoutable* and also

upwards to smash the deck beneath the Frenchmen's feet. Lucas, with his ship splintered and shattered beneath his feet, still hung onto his prey like a terrier at the throat of a bulldog. As hundreds of cheering Frenchmen rushed to board *Victory*, the British *Téméraire*, a three decker of 98 guns, appeared out of the smoke and sandwiched the little *Redoutable* between herself and *Victory*. Her upper guns fired a broadside killing about 200 Frenchmen. Unable now to fight, Lucas would not surrender and he threatened to burn his ship. Finally a boarding party from *Téméraire* took the *Redoutable*. This was the scene that was taking place while Nelson was dying on the orlop deck of *Victory*.

OFF CAPE TRAFALGAR, 4.30 P.M. ON 21 OCTOBER 1805. Silence had at last descended and the smoke cleared. The British ships and their prizes floated helplessly, many of them dismasted and with shattered hulls. Nelson and 448 British were dead, and 1,217 were wounded. Of the French and Spanish 4,408 were dead, 2,545 wounded and about 20,000 were prisoners. The heart of Napoleon's Navy had been broken and once again the threat of imminent invasion was gone.

Heavy winds caused storm conditions for the next three weeks and many of the dearly bought prizes were lost. Men struggled to keep afloat broken wrecks that were worth a small fortune in prize money, but to no avail. Later a grant from Parliament of £300,000 eased their loss. Most captains received about £3,000, lieutenants about £226, gunners about £150, midshipmen £37 and seamen £6.

left: *left to right, Vice-Admiral Pierre Villeneuve, 1763–1806, who commanded the Franco-Spanish fleet at Trafalgar; Admiral Horatio Nelson, 1758–1805, and Admiral Cuthbert Collingwood, 1750–1810, who took command of the British fleet after Nelson's death.*

right: *The loss of a ship-of-the-line on blockade, painted by J. C. Schetky, in 1804. The ship has been driven onto the rocks and is being abandoned.*

The watch goes on

The battle off Cape Trafalgar was a decisive victory and the British took care to hold on to the advantage it gave them. The war was not over. France still had a strong fleet scattered around the ports of Europe. Her shipyards were still producing excellent ships at an alarming rate. To the Admiralty, studying the overall situation, it was clear that the threat of invasion had certainly been postponed but not completely eliminated. No one could foresee the future and it looked as if the war might continue for another fifty years. There was to be no let up. The blockade had to go on with every effort being made to draw the French out to sea and destroy them.

Outside Europe hundreds of French privateers were scattered over the oceans ready to pounce on merchant ships and sometimes even British frigates. The convoy system had to continue.

Single-ship actions and battles involving small squadrons took place as before, but for the large fleets the wearisome blockade dragged on. The effects of the constant watch on a man such as Admiral Collingwood were typical, and resulted from the determination of the Admiralty to maintain the blockade. Collingwood was at heart a quiet family man who longed for retirement; his dream was to tend his gardens at home in Morpeth. He had joined the Navy when eleven years old and of his forty-four years as a seaman he had only spent four ashore. After Trafalgar he commanded the fleet in the Mediterranean and spent his time patrolling hostile coasts. As his tiredness increased, he asked the Admiralty to replace him, but they had no one else with the right combination of qualities for this difficult task. In 1810, utterly exhausted, he died at sea.

Collingwood was not the only casualty of the dangerous watch. Thousands of men and hundreds of ships were lost as disease, shipwreck, personal accidents, rotting wood and accidental explosions took their toll. The decay of the ships caused by rotting oak was a serious problem to which there was no easy solution. In the old style of warfare ships were refitted in the winter after the summer battles. Now ships were in action all year round since the Admiralty needed every ship at sea to keep up the blockade. Napoleon could perhaps be excused for having told Villeneuve that the British Navy would wear itself out by attempting an all-the-year-round blockade. It *was* wearing the Navy down – in men, ships, and morale – but the Admiralty would not let up. The watch must go on, regardless.

7   TAKING THE OFFENSIVE

1805–1807

With the enemy fleets avoiding head-on clashes, the only large-scale offensive open to the British fleets was to co-operate with the army in landing troops on foreign shores. In January 1806, 6,000 troops were landed at Cape Town, and, in September, Buenos Aires in the Argentine was attacked, while a British force was ferried to Hanover – then ferried back again. Troops were landed in Sicily and Naples. The Naples division had to be withdrawn but a garrison remained in Sicily and from there raids were made on the coast of Italy. These events, and many similar actions, confirmed that Britain controlled the seas. The Admiralty was capable of carrying troops to any part of the world and could maintain an unbroken supply-line to them.

The year 1807 saw Napoleon more powerful than ever on land. He had subjugated Austria and Prussia and won over Russia to his side. All of Europe was under orders to cease any trading with Britain. Now the Danish fleet in Copenhagen, comprising fifteen ships-of-the-line and thirty smaller ships, was about to come under French control. To prevent this a force of 18,000 men sailed from Britain to Denmark and at Vedbock on 16 August they swarmed ashore under cover of the fleet's guns. By 7 September Copenhagen had surrendered and the Danish fleet was in British hands.

The capture of the Danish fleet added even more strength to the British Navy, but it was only a pin-prick against the armed might of France. In November 1807 French troops crossed from Spain into Portugal; the whole of the Atlantic coast of Europe was now in enemy hands. Napoleon prohibited all

The Capture of Mauritius, 1810. A typical landing of British troops seen from the deck of the most inshore transport ship. The warships and transports would anchor as close as possible to the shore and the troops would be ferried ashore in smaller boats. Sloops and pinnaces would approach closer inshore to give covering fire if necessary. Many of the leading boats would have 9-pounder cannons in their bows. Once the troops were safely ashore, stores, equipment and horses were ferried to land.

trade with Britain, and Britain prevented anyone trading with Europe. It was stalemate. Only armies could break the deadlock and decide the issue.

Spain and Portugal

In 1808 the first real opportunity arose for British troops to operate on a large scale in Europe. The Spanish were now in revolt against the French and they appealed for aid. The Portuguese, too, hated the French occupying forces, so it seemed that here at last was an area for a real offensive. In August, British transports, supported by battleships, arrived off Mondego Bay in Portugal and soon soldiers, horses, artillery, and supplies were ferried ashore. Led by Sir Arthur Wellesley, a force of 13,000 men, with more to come in the months ahead, had landed in Europe with the promise of support from the local people.

So began the campaign known as the Peninsular War that was to last until 1813. For four years the Navy shuttled back and forth, ferrying out troops, food, ammunition and supplies, and sailing back with prisoners and wounded. Frigates scuttled up and down the coast acting as spies and messengers for the army.

In 1809 they had the less heartening task of using 250 transports and a squadron of battleships to evacuate hurriedly thousands of retreating British troops from La Coruña in north-west Spain. But the rest of the army fought on under their brilliant commander Wellesley, later Lord Wellington.

Wellington's successes in Spain and Portugal turned everyone's attention to the army. News of victories was now all about battles on land. The Navy's role was vital but not obvious any more. From 1808 onwards the main offensive role of the British Navy was in combined operations with the army.

WALCHEREN: THE EXPEDITION THAT FAILED. On 28 July 1809 over 32,000 British troops and cavalry were shipped to the mouth of the River Scheldt using 400 transports and twenty-nine ships-of-the-line with their lower decks cleared to carry the large number of men. The flotilla was protected by eight ships-of-the-line, twenty-three frigates, five bomb vessels and about fifty smaller types of warships.

The aim was to land the troops, who would then move on Antwerp and destroy the important shipbuilding yards, arsenal and port there. The landings went well, but the army's move-

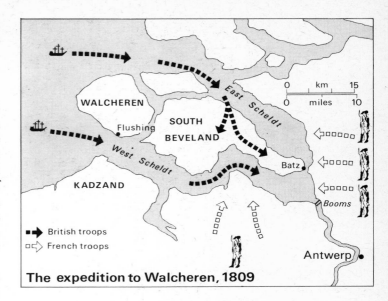

The expedition to Walcheren, 1809

ments were slow and it was not until four weeks later that the islands of Walcheren and South Beveland were properly occupied. The town of Flushing had to be hammered into submission with a two-day-long bombardment by naval vessels. Six hundred civilians were killed in the bombardment and half the town was destroyed.

By the time the army was ready to cross from Batz to the mainland masses of French troops were arriving and strong fortifications had been built. Fever began to take a heavy toll of the troops and in the last days of August the Navy embarked the whole expedition and returned home.

Out of the 4,000 men who died on the expedition only 1,000 were killed by enemy action. The rest died of fever. However, no ships were lost and the expedition returned to England with 5,450 prisoners.

Controversial tactics and machines

The war years saw thousands killed violently on land and sea, often in savage hand-to-hand fighting. But certain conventions of gallantry and fair play did exist. Prisoners of war were usually treated with some consideration and even friendliness, though the quality of consideration was naturally related to the social standing of the captive. Captured seamen often fed with

Two fireships bearing down on an anchored squadron. While the ships burn, probably soon to explode, rockets lashed to the tops shoot off in all directions. The picture is from Congreve's own book describing his rocket system.

their captors while captured officers, provided they gave their parole, were allowed the freedom of the ship. Many a British captain entertained his one time enemy at his home in England. Soldiers and sailors were supposed to fight openly and honourably, so traitors and spies, although employed by the government, were detested by all fighting men. There were also some devices, both new inventions and old ideas revived, that did not fit in with such gentlemanly codes.

ROCKETS. Colonel (later Sir) William Congreve developed the use of rockets as incendiaries and to carry canister shot. They were in general use throughout the army and navy, but were considered a joke by most serving men. The effect of rockets was often more frightening than dangerous and their flight was so unpredictable that they could even reverse direction and land behind their starting point. They did, however, play a large and destructive part in the bombardment of Copenhagen in 1807 and the attack on Flushing in 1809. They probably did more harm to helpless civilians than to soldiers or seamen.

FIRESHIPS. The British had used fireships since the sixteenth century and during the Napoleonic Wars they had refined their construction and use to a fine art. The French considered them unethical and made it clear that captured crews of fireships would face a firing squad.

Fireships were usually old single-deck ships that had been stripped of all useful equipment. Narrow wooden gutters or channels were laid fore and aft on the bare gun deck planking and then similar guttering was laid athwartships across them.

Barrels of resin, powder, and turpentine were placed in each of the open squares formed by the crossed guttering and trains of quick burning fuses were put in the channels leading from the powder to the stern of the ship. The whole was then loosely covered with wood shavings and tarred canvas, leaving plenty of ventilation. Large ports were cut into the ship's side to provide a through draught and thick tarred rope ran from the powder, through the ports, and up into the sails and rigging. This was the basic fireship; it could be converted into an explosive ship by placing mortar shells on each powder keg and stowing hundreds of grenades at suitable points. As a final touch Congreve rockets could be lashed to the spars and rigging.

The ship, manned by volunteers, was sailed as normal until the last possible moment and then the sails were set and the wheel lashed to hold it on a steady course. The crew hurried into the small boat towed astern, leaving the lieutenant to light the fire that would light the train of fuses. Once he had lit the fire the lieutenant had about fifteen minutes before the ship erupted into a blazing furnace, so he wasted no time in clambering into the boat and getting clear of the ship. Many lieutenants simply dived through the stern windows and swam to the waiting boat.

MINES. William Richardson, from South Shields, was a gunner in 1809, and described in his own words a new invention:

'Received from the Berwick cutter six copper submarine carcasses some to hold 540 lb [245 kg] of powder, and others 405 lbs [184 kg]; they were intended to sink a ship, and be used as follows. Suppose a light rope about six fathoms long be stretched across the head of a ship, and one carcasse fastened to one end and another to the other; then lower them down in the water by buoy ropes to each about 21 ft [6.4 m] for a line-of-battle ship, and then let them hang by cork buoys; and when let go they will drift with the tide towards the ship, suspended in that manner, and when the middle part of the six fathom rope gets over the ship's cable it brings the carcasses round, and they swing under the ship's bilgeway: there is a piece of clockwork, watertight, fixed to each which you must set to the number of minutes you suppose it to require in reaching the ship's bottom. It then blows up, and tis said, will blow a hole in a line-of-battle ship's bottom. We never tried them – indeed, our Admiral said it was not fair proceeding.'

FULTON'S SUBMARINE. Robert Fulton was an American pacifist who believed he had invented a weapon that would make sea-warfare impossible. In 1797 he approached the French Directory with his plans for a vessel that could sail under water and plant explosive charges under warships. Although interest was shown, it was not until Napoleon Bonaparte came to power that Fulton received funds and help to build his submarine, called *Nautilus*. In 1800 it underwent its first trials and successfully blew up the target vessel in the River Seine. Plans were made to try it against a blockading British ship off Brest but Admirals Villaret-Joyeuse and Latouche-Tréville thought that his invention was a despicable means of warfare and refused to allow him to proceed.

In 1804 Fulton tried to interest the British and again a practical demonstration destroyed the target ship. Like their French counterparts the Admiralty condemned the weapon on moral grounds, though it is possible that they realised that the development of such a weapon could destroy British sea superiority.

Cost and profit

Despite the early doubts about their capabilities, British troops Wellington cleared the French from Spain and Portugal, one of the many allied armies that closed in on 1815 they and their allies fought to victory at royed Napoleon's last hopes. As a British one-time master of Europe to exile in the south Atlantic the victors could turn to clearing up the aftermath of twenty-two years of war.

The Admiralty could claim with confidence that their strategy had produced the desired results. There had been continuous naval activity throughout the war: they had swept the sea clear of enemy fleets, and maintained control of the oceans despite all efforts to wrest it from them. They had successfully blockaded thousands of miles of hostile shore and even harrassed the enemy inside his own ports. The policy of 'open blockade' had tempted enemy ships into the open seas and there many had been destroyed. British ships had carried the army to Europe and had ferried essential supplies. Naval officers boasted that it was their ships that had beaten Napoleon, and there were few who contradicted them.

In 1815 the ocean-going merchant and war fleets of the rest of the world were either destroyed or considerably reduced. British sea-power was supreme. Brittannia ruled the waves and was to do so for another hundred years.

Victory at sea had not been achieved without cost. In the early years the Admiralty had demanded money and men. Quick successes enabled them to ask for more money and men which in turn laid the foundation for more successes. Taxes rose and the press-gangs were detested by the civilian population, but to balance this they could cheer each new sea victory and make heroes out of admirals such as Collingwood and Nelson or daring frigate captains like Blackwood. Grim news from the mainland of Europe could always be alleviated by cheering reports of British naval success. The Navy could do little wrong in the public eye.

British ships were sunk or captured by the French, but naval activity was so energetic and so wide in scope that gains well outweighed losses. Figures are difficult to assess but it appears that the final estimate (not including ships below the size of a frigate) of British ships lost to the French was one 74, one 54, and eight frigates, a total of ten ships. (Remember that many British ships had been captured and then retaken at some later date and that these are not included in the final estimate.)

The French and their allies lost an estimated 139 ships-of-the-line and 229 frigates to the British, a total of 368 ships.

The confident and aggressive attitude of the British, and their concentration on expert gunnery to hammer at the enemy hull in order to destroy guns and men, seemed to have produced the best results. Their Lordships in the Admiralty, receiving the

news of recent engagements, must have been very satisfied as they read the results and casualty lists. The sample lists that follow show how gunnery and tactics favoured the British:

8 JUNE 1796. Single-ship action: *Unicorn*, 32 guns, in a ten-hour running fight off Scilly Islands with the French *Tribune*, 36 guns. *Tribune* was captured:
French losses, 37 killed and 15 wounded.
British losses, nil.

4 NOVEMBER 1805. A small fleet action off Finistère. British victory. French ships captured:
Formidable, 84 guns, Rear-Admiral Dumanoir:
200 killed and wounded.
Duguay-Trouin, 74 guns, Captain Touffet: 150 killed and wounded.
Mont Blanc, 74 guns, Captain Villegris: 180 killed and wounded.
Scipion, 74 guns, Captain Berenger: 200 killed and wounded.

British casualties:
Caesar, 80 guns, 4 killed, 24 wounded.
Namur, 74 guns, 4 killed, 8 wounded.
Hero, 74 guns: 10 killed, 15 wounded.
Courageux, 74 guns: 1 killed, 13 wounded.
Santa Margarita, 36 guns: 1 killed, 6 wounded.
Phoenix, 36 guns: 2 killed, 6 wounded.

In the Admiralty's overall strategy the most important single decision was to establish the blockade – the watch. The tactic of keeping well away to tempt the enemy out into the open could become a dangerous gamble. If the blockading admiral misjudged or was driven off station by the weather then the Admiralty had to depend on its reserve strategy of recalling all outlying fleets and ships to the Channel approaches in order to make a barrier against the oncoming foe. The Admiralty also had to place all its trust in the good judgement of the men it had appointed to command the ships and fleets. Until Trafalgar no one was absolutely sure that it would work. It did work but the cost was high.

The Admiralty's world strategy of convoy work, the watch and operations in the East and West Indies had a price. The number of seamen lost by direct enemy action was ab
– but the losses due to disease, accident and ship
nearly 93,000; 334 ships were lost by shipwreck

It had cost nearly 100,000 men but
calculated the odds correctly – and wor

48